52
FANTASTIC
DATES
FOR YOU
AND YOUR
MATE

OTHER BOOKS
BY THE AUTHORS

10 Great Dates to Energize Your Marriage

10 Great Dates for Empty Nesters

10 Great Dates Before You Say
"I Do" (with Curt and Natelle Brown)

No Time for Sex

The Second Half of Marriage

Fighting for Your Empty Nest Marriage
(with Howard Markman, Scott Stanley,
and Susan Blumberg)

Loving Your Relative—Even When
You Don't See Eye-to-Eye
(with John and Margaret Bell)

New Baby Stress

Marriage Moments

Family Moments

Quiet Whispers from God's Heart for Couples

Answering the 8 Cries of the Spirited Child

Suddenly They're 13!—or the Art of Hugging a Cactus

52 FANTASTIC DATES FOR YOU AND YOUR MATE

DAVID & CLAUDIA ARP

NELSON BOOKS
A Division of Thomas Nelson Publishers
Since 1798

www.thomasnelson.com

Published in Nashville, Tennessee, by Thomas Nelson, Inc.

Nelson Books titles may be purchased in bulk for educational, business, fundraising, or sales promotional use. For information, please
email SpecialMarkets@ThomasNelson.com.

Library of Congress Cataloging-in-Publication Data

Arp, Dave.
   52 fantastic dates for you and your mate / David and Claudia
   Arp.
     p. cm.
   ISBN 978-0-7852-9728-4
   1. Marriage—Religious aspects—Christianity. 2. Dating (Social
customs)—Religious aspects—Christianity. 3. Dating (Social customs). I. Title: Fifty-two fantastic dates for you and your mate. II.
Arp, Claudia. III. Title.
   BV835.A77 2005
   306.872—dc22

                                                    2004018015

Printed in the United States of America

04 05 06 07 08 QW 9 8 7 6 5 4 3 2 1

To couples everywhere
who want to add fun to their marriage
through dating.

———

We are grateful to our friends, family members,
and participants in our Marriage Alive seminars
who shared their creative dates with us so we could
pass them on to you.

Special thanks to Janie Johnson for her help and to
Janet Thoma and Susan Salmon for their excellent
editorial guidance; and to the in-house staff of Thomas
Nelson who made writing this book fun for us.

If this book inspires you to date your mate, we would love to hear from you. Tell us your most fun experiences. You can contact us through our Web site at www.marriagealive.com.

If you like these dates, you'll find more ideas in our *10 Great Dates* series:

10 Great Dates Before You Say "I Do"
10 Great Dates to Energize Your Marriage
10 Great Dates for Empty Nesters

For more information go to www.marriagealive.com.

Let us encourage you to go on and date your mate. It will keep your marriage alive, fun, and headed in the right direction!

CONTENTS

———

DO-IT-TOGETHER DATES

CHEAP-AND-EASY DATES

"WE'RE JUST TOO TIRED" DATES

FOREWORD

"Many view marriage as death, boredom, or the end of the line," a marriage specialist said on a recent television talk show. It made us stop and question, "Why are people frightened of marriage? Why do some view it as the 'end of the line'?"

Having worked with married couples for many years, we have our own opinion. We believe life goes out of a marriage when the couple stops working on it. To take it a step further, we have observed that when a couple stops working on their marriage, they stop having fun together. Show us a marriage that is faltering, and we'll show you a marriage where the fun is gone.

And where the fun is gone, there is a mighty good chance they don't date their mate! Dating is something they did before they got married. It is not in their marriage vocabulary today.

In the following pages, we want to do something about that. We offer you *52 Fantastic Dates for You and Your Mate*. Unlike books you read from cover to cover, you can read this book spontaneously. Simply read the section that suits your present mood; then choose a date from that section. Remember, this is a resource to enrich your relationship with each other.

This book is divided into seven parts, each offering a different category of dates. You'll find everything from Romantic Dates to Getting-in-Shape Dates to Cheap-and-

Easy Dates. We especially recommend the "We're Just Too Tired" Dates for those times you think you're just too exhausted to date your mate.

We want to emphasize that all the dates in this book have been done by someone, somewhere! A big thank-you to all those who shared their creative dates with us. Many are alumni from our Marriage Alive seminars all around the country. From Washington State to Florida, they happily pass their fun times on to you.

Will dating make a difference in your marriage? Our answer is an emphatic "Yes!" If you don't believe us, ask Fred and Nancy. Here's what they wrote us:

"Thank you for sharing your dating ideas. My husband and I have a lot of fun in our marriage and it is legal, moral, and inexpensive. We know we can't take our marriage for granted, so we continue to search for reinforcements such as your books."

Fred and Nancy, here is the next installment! This book is for you and for all who want to make their marriages come alive with fun, laughter, and good times together. The ball is in your court. Go on and have a great time dating your mate!

JUST-FOR-FUN DATES

FORMAL-
DINNER-
IN-THE-PARK
DATE

THE IDEA:

Formal dinners don't have to be stuffy and don't have to be crowded affairs. Actually, the guest list can include only two—you and your mate. There is no real protocol for this date. It's completely open-ended but our friends, Larry and Lois, tell us it's a ball.

MAKE YOUR MATE FEEL LIKE A STAR:

Most everyone has been to a picnic in a park—complete with paper plates, cold fried chicken, plenty of people, and ants and other bugs. But very few have attended a private black-tie affair out under the stars. This is one date, if you pull it off, that will make your mate feel like a star celebrity.

CHOOSE THE RIGHT SETTING:

Choose a park that lends itself to the romantic, like one with a waterfall, statues, or maybe a lake. It's easy to convert a picnic table into a formal dining room, or you can bring your own folding table and chairs. You'll also need to bring your favorite tablecloth, linen napkins, china, and silverware. A

1

vase of fresh flowers (wildflowers are ideal) and a candelabra will add to the formal atmosphere.

If you are industrious, you can prepare food beforehand and grill in the park (if allowed). Or if you want to simplify, call your favorite restaurant and order take-out dinners. Another option is to pick up dinner from the deli of your favorite gourmet grocery store.

DRESS FOR THE OCCASION:

You will want to dress accordingly. Put on your tux or formal gown if you already own one, but prepare yourself for a few stares. If you don't want to go that formal, a coat and tie or dress is fine and will still add to the formality of the evening.

Take along a CD player with your favorite music CDs to add to the atmosphere. If you feel nostalgic, we suggest oldies music from your premarriage dates. If you're looking for something fresh and romantic in an outdoorsy way, we recommend:

- ◆ A favorite classical recording.
- ◆ George Winston (piano and instrumental from Windom Hill).
- ◆ Michael Hedges (wonderful acoustic guitar).
- ◆ Norah Jones or Diana Krall (blues and jazz).
- ◆ Gipsy Kings (for a fun Latin flair).

This might be just the opportunity to surprise your date

with a new CD—one that will remind you of your Formal-Dinner-in-the-Park Date.

CONSIDER ALTERNATIVES:
An option for those who do not live near a park: one couple we know set up a table, complete with tablecloth and candles on their front walk. Not only did they experience a unique and fun dinner—they also provided their neighbors with a new topic of conversation and laughter.

2

PHOTO DATE

THE IDEA:

We love pictures! In fact, we spent the first year of our empty nest going through all our pictures, framing and hanging the special ones.

Perhaps you've heard of a "Wailing Wall." Well, we have a "Wedding Wall," with pictures dating back to our parents as well as pictures of our three married sons. Actually it was our last family wedding that instigated our Photo Dates. Looking at honeymoon pictures, we were amazed at how many pictures our son and new daughter-in-law had of just the two of them. When we asked who took the pictures, we discovered they were the photographers. They simply set the timer on their camera and ran and posed for their self-portraits.

LEARN TO DO IT RIGHT:

At the next opportunity, we had our own Photo Date. We didn't have immediate success. We didn't even know how to set the timer on our camera! When we finally figured it out, we didn't always focus it right. Only the two of us know who the black shadows are in some of the pictures. But we did have fun in the process and are continuing to fine-tune our

4

Photo Dates. Digital cameras have only added to our fun. Now we can have instant gratification and know that we have the pose we want. Also, we can print them out when we get home from our Photo Date. Plan your own Photo Date today. Trust us, it's fun!

ADAPT THE DATE FOR YOU:
Whatever kind of camera you have, you can adapt this date to your own situation. If you have a camera with a timer, all the better. If not, you can buy inexpensive extension cables to trigger the camera for couple self-portraits. Just remember, for every great shot you take, you'll shoot four or five others. With a digital camera, you can simply delete the ones you don't like.

KEEP YOUR COSTS DOWN:
The cost of developing film or printing pictures from your digital camera has come down in recent years. Research your own area and find the cheapies. Look for discount coupons in your local newspaper or special deals at your grocery store. Our favorite and cheapest place (for developing film from our 36 mm camera) also offers one-hour service, which is great for those of us who like immediate gratification!

If you don't have a camera with a timer, or don't even have a camera, you can pick up an inexpensive disposable camera (which includes film) for about five dollars. Even adding the cost of developing, your date should not cost more than ten dollars, which makes this date a Cheap-and-Easy Date too.

Go to your favorite haunts and snap away. You may even be able to recruit an unsuspecting person to snap a picture of the two of you together.

You can extend the fun of this date by making your own memory scrapbook. You'll be cataloging memories together. Picture that!

3
OWL-WATCHING DATE

THE IDEA:
The Owl-Watching Date may be the most unique date we've heard about.

While participating in a Book Fest, we picked up this creative date from a fellow author, Fred Alsop. Sitting with other authors in the "signing well" and waiting for the autograph seekers to arrive gave us the opportunity to visit with Fred. Our standard question, "What is your favorite date?" received anything but a standard answer. Fred's suggestion? Have an Owl-Watching Date! Looking for owls on a moonlit night, he tried to convince us, can be romantic as well as fun.

PREPARE FOR THE NIGHT:
Now, we promised you that someone has actually done each of our fifty-two dates, and Fred swore he had done the Owl-Watching Date many, many times. His suggestions included the following:

- ◆ Choose a moonlit, warm night with no time limitations.
- ◆ Find a quiet place. The more secluded the location the better, but Fred told us if you are a city

slicker, you can do this date in your own backyard or local park.

◆ Be patient. Sometimes owls will appear in as few
as twenty minutes. Sometimes you may need to
wait several hours. But it's amazing, he told us,
how being alone together in the dark, out in
nature, causes wonderful conversations to happen. Subjects you haven't talked about for years
may surface. Simple things remembered are
likely to bring a closeness that just doesn't happen in the hustle and bustle of the day.

◆ To increase your chance of seeing owls, try imi-
tating them. To illustrate, Fred gave us a pierc-
ing screech owl call. (We'll have to practice that
one.)

◆ To learn more about owls, or other birds as well,
pick up and study a book on birds. If you live in
the southeastern part of the United States, we
recommend Fred's book, *Birds of the Smokies*
(Great Smoky Mountain Natural History
Association: Gatlinburg, TN, 1991).

◆ To top off your Owl-Watching Date, here's one
last suggestion from Fred: as the sun comes up,
cook breakfast together.

We're not real outdoorsy people, but this is one date we
just may try. Since Dave's a "night owl" and Claudia's a "day
lark," we at least would see a couple of "birds." Who knows
what other fun things we might find to do!

GOURMET-COOKING DATE

THE IDEA:

Some dates you have before you get married seem to be natural dates after you get married too. Our own married kids have proven this in our family. We've even been the recipients of their Gourmet-Cooking Dates. This Arp date has a history.

When our kids were in college, their funds for gourmet restaurants were limited, but their taste for fine cuisine was not! So they began to cook their own gourmet dinners. A fun Arp tradition evolved. Whenever our sons had college friends to visit in our home, they sequestered their unsuspecting guests into culinary duty. Whoever was visiting (male or female) joined forces with our kids and cooked a special dinner. One of their friends turned out to be a first-class chef.

CHOOSE A THEME:

Sometimes these dinners had themes. We never knew quite what to expect—like the time our kids did an Oriental dinner. They served us on the screened porch on a quilt surrounded by plants. We felt as if we were in an Oriental garden.

Have Fun Breaking Tradition:

The most memorable gourmet meal from our kids was the Christmas their gift to us was to prepare the entire Christmas dinner. That year tradition was out and gourmet was in. It was an experience we won't soon forget. They cooked straight through the night on Christmas Eve. Have you ever tried to sleep to the smells and sounds of someone making homemade manicotti?

You Can Plan Your Dinner:

If you have never had a Gourmet-Cooking Date and are interested in trying one, here are a few pointers:

- ◆ Choose recipes you've never cooked before. A good source of recipes can be found in such magazines as *Gourmet* or *Bon Appetit*. You can have a fun preliminary date reading all those cookbooks you got as wedding presents or purchased through fund-raisers.
- ◆ Together make out your grocery list. You may want to set a budget for your meal, but go on and be a little extravagant. It definitely will be a cheaper date than going to an exclusive gourmet restaurant.
- ◆ Grocery shop together. This can be another fun preliminary date.
- ◆ While this is a fun Just-for-Two Date, you may want to turn it into an even more productive date by pulling off the Dinner-Party Date (see Date 27).

CHOOSE FROM OUR FAMILY FAVORITES:
Here are some of our family's favorite sources of recipes:

◆ *Pasta Fresca,* by Viana La Place and Evan Kleiman (New York: William Morrow, 2001).

◆ *Cucina Rustica,* by Viana La Place and Evan Kleiman (New York: William Morrow, 2001).

◆ *Sundays at Moosewood Restaurant,* by Moosewood Collective (New York: Simon & Schuster, 1990).

◆ *The Vegetarian Epicure Book Two,* by Anna Thomas (New York: Alfred A. Knopf, 1978).

◆ *Cuisine Rapide,* by Pierre Franey and Bryan Miller (New York: Three Rivers Press, 2001).

◆ Cookbooks by Pierre Franey including: *The New York Times 60 Minute Gourmet* (New York: Three Rivers Press, 2000).

Here is an Arp family favorite recipe that is very easy to prepare:

Italiano Marinara

2 tablespoons olive oil

1 medium onion, chopped

2 cloves garlic, minced (More garlic actually added zest!)

3 28-oz. cans tomatoes, undrained

2 tablespoons chopped fresh parsley (If you use dried parsley, add more.)

1 teaspoon sugar

2 teaspoons basil

½ teaspoon oregano

½ teaspoon salt

½ teaspoon fresh ground pepper

1 package (8 oz.) spaghetti, uncooked

1 cup (4 oz.) shredded mozzarella cheese

In a 2-quart saucepan heat oil and cook onion and garlic until tender but not brown. Stir in tomatoes with liquid, parsley, sugar, basil, oregano, salt and pepper; bring to a boil then reduce heat and simmer, stirring occasionally to break up tomatoes, 15–20 minutes. Meanwhile, cook spaghetti according to package directions; drain. Toss spaghetti with sauce and place in 1-quart casserole. Top with mozzarella cheese and broil 3 minutes or until cheese is melted.

Makes 4 servings.

BUBBLE
DATE

THE IDEA:

Sometimes our neighbors worry about us! On this day they were really concerned. "What are the Arps up to now?" they asked, as they watched humongous bubbles floating over the roof of our house.

"Not to worry," we could have told them. We were simply having a Bubble Date!

One perk (or liability) of our work in marriage and family enrichment is we get to try out ideas before passing them on to others. That's how we came to have a Bubble Date. But it was so much fun, we have repeated it several times.

A friend put a bug in our ears that blowing bubbles—big bubbles—was lots of fun. We did have positive childhood memories of little plastic containers of liquid and the fun of making bubbles, so we decided to give the big bubbles a try. You can too!

GET WHAT YOU NEED:

The equipment is simple. You can pick up large commercial bubble wands in toy stores. They come in an assortment of astrobright colors and sizes. Or you can make your own wands out of coat hangers.

FOLLOW THE RECIPE:

Make your own bubble mixture with this simple recipe:

Bubble Fun

Combine:
2 cups liquid detergent
¼ cup corn syrup
6 cups water

Put bubble mixture in a large shallow pan—like a roasting pan. Dip the bubble wand and wave through the air. You'll have wonderful large bubbles everywhere. You also can use a kitchen funnel. Dip the large end of the funnel into the bubble mixture and blow through the small end.

TAKE THE IDEA EVERYWHERE:

By the way, this is definitely an Out-of-Doors Date and one you'll find yourself wanting to repeat. It's especially fun at the beach. You can watch as the beach winds take your bubbles to parts unknown.

There's a child in each of us. Be willing to let your child out from time to time. It will add laughter and fun to your marriage team.

6

COUPON DATE

Dr. Scott Peck, in his classic best-selling book, *The Road Less Traveled* (New York: Simon & Schuster, 1978), says a sign of maturity is to be able to delay gratification. The Coupon Date lets you do just that—but you get to have fun in the process.

Remember all those fun things you occasionally talk about but never get around to doing? Now is an opportunity to put some feet on those good ideas. Or perhaps you want to do something fun together but have difficulty coming up with anything to do. If this fits you, we just may have the solution to your dilemma. Have a Coupon Date!

THE IDEA:

Coupon Dates began to appear at the Arps' when our children were very young. We were so busy with family, careers, and life that our date times together were practically nonexistent. We decided to do something about it by having a Coupon Date.

Just what is a Coupon Date? It's a date to come up with future dates—thus Dr. Peck's "delayed gratification." But it is also fun.

BRAINSTORM DATE IDEAS:

Part of the fun of dating your mate is the anticipation factor—looking forward to the things you are going to do together. Here's how to begin.

1. Choose a time when you won't be interrupted for a couple of hours. You may want to go out for breakfast or coffee and dessert. Take along pen and paper and your imagination.

2. You can draw from our fifty-two date suggestions or come up with others, like these:

   ◆ Go roller-skating.
   ◆ Fly kites together.
   ◆ Catch your favorite movie.
   ◆ Watch the sunset, sunrise, etc.
   ◆ Fill in with your own idea:

   _____

3. Now make the date coupons. Here's what you need:

Index cards	Hole puncher
Colored markers	Yarn

Punch a hole in each card. (If you are artsy, you can decorate each card.) Write out one date idea for each coupon. Tie coupons together with yarn, and presto, you have a coupon book for future dates. Also, you can design them on your computer and print them out.

ONE FINAL SUGGESTION:
Hang your coupon book in a conspicuous place, perhaps in the kitchen so you will see it often. It will be a reminder of fun times ahead. Who says delayed gratification isn't fun? Not us, but this is one date you won't want to delay.

BOOK DATE

THE IDEA:

Two of our favorite activities are eating and reading, so when we discovered a bookstore that served food, we knew we had hit the jackpot. More and more bookstores are becoming innovative in what they offer, so check out the bookstores in your local area.

One bookstore we know offers poetry readings. Another of our favorite bookstores offers unique opportunities, like mini-workshops on travel or autograph sessions with authors. They also offer story time for children. We know couples who take their young children to story time and then have fun browsing through books while their little ones are happily entertained.

READING YOU CAN DO TOGETHER:

Another couple, Nan and Randy, enjoy reading the same book or chapter and then discussing it when they go out for breakfast or dinner. If you are looking for books to read together that will enrich your life and marriage, consider the following:

- ◆ *The Love List*, by Les and Leslie Parrott (Grand Rapids, MI: Zondervan, 2002).
- ◆ *10 Great Dates to Energize Your Marriage*, by

David and Claudia Arp (Grand Rapids, MI: Zondervan, 1997).

◆ *Fighting for Your Marriage*, by Howard Markman, Scott Stanley, and Susan Blumberg (San Francisco: Jossey-Bass, 2001).

◆ *Loving Your Relatives: Even When You Don't See Eye-to-Eye*, by John and Margaret Bell and David and Claudia Arp (Carol Stream, IL: Tyndale, 2003).

◆ *No Time for Sex*, by David and Claudia Arp (West Monroe, LA: Howard Publishing, 2004).

◆ *Empowering Couples*, by David and Amy Olson (Minneapolis: Life Innovations, Inc., 2000).

◆ *Men Are from Mars, Women Are from Venus*, by John Gray (New York: Quill, 2004).

◆ *The Seven Principles for Making Marriage Work*, by John Gottman and Nan Silver (New York: Three Rivers Press, 2000).

A TIP:
If your local bookstore doesn't have some of the titles, you can find them at www.amazon.com.

This is one date that not only is fun, but can pump some fresh air into your marital tires. It's your turn to prove that we are right. Go on and book your Book Date. Trust us. You won't be disappointed.

8

YELLOW-ROAD, BLUE-HIGHWAYS DATE

Dave's travel motto is "Why travel on the interstate if there is a cute yellow road you can take?" Claudia's travel motto is "How quickly can we get there, and which is the most direct route?" Obviously, we have very different travel perspectives, but there is one time we do agree. It's when we have a Yellow-Road Date!

THE IDEA:
What's a yellow road? Dave's little yellow roads became famous when we were living in Austria. Whenever we traveled, he always wanted to take the scenic route. We soon learned that on the Austrian maps, yellow roads meant scenery—gorgeous scenery! We also learned that yellow roads could mean narrow roads (as in room for one car on a mountain ledge) or gravel roads. On one unforgettable occasion, it meant a cow path. Traveling Austria's yellow roads in our American station wagon was very interesting. We still wonder how we were able to navigate some of them.

Over the years of traveling yellow roads we have seen a lot of beautiful country, so we confidently recommend this date to you, especially since another couple, Brenda and Mike, made the same dating suggestion. They actually called their date a Blue-Highways Date, which they named for the book by William Least Heat-Moon, *Blue Highways*. Here are their tips on how to have a Blue-Highways Date.

PLAN TO TRAVEL THE BACK ROADS:

1. Consider how much time you have for your Blue-Highways Date. Brenda and Mike suggest a minimum of one day. If you can make it an overnight or weekend, all the better.

2. Choose the area you'd like to explore. For instance, in California, it might be the San Bernardino Mountains or Redwood Forest; in New York, the Catskills; or in Colorado, the Rockies. It could even be a forty-mile radius around your own hometown.

3. Go to an unfamiliar area and take the little blue roads. No interstate travel or four-lane roads are allowed.

4. Resist the urge to stop at fast-food or chain restaurants. See what you can discover, and stop at any interesting place you find.

DISCOVER NEW TERRITORIES:
You never know what you may find. Brenda and Mike said they've discovered everything from pig races to barbecues. Once, they even stopped for a square dance.

We've stumbled on to wonderful museums, parks, nature trails, antique shops, and junk stores. Did you know that in the mountains of North Carolina, they even have "woolly worm races"? It's an annual event and people come from all over. We've also found quaint little bed-and-breakfasts and property where we would love to build a mountain cabin. (That's for our fantasy date!)

Perhaps the most enjoyable is the beautiful scenery we've discovered. Sometimes we just like to get out of the car, sit on a rock or log, and realize how thankful we are for this unique, beautiful world and for each other. Maybe we should retitle this date The Grateful Date. Try it and see if you both agree!

GETTING-IN-SHAPE DATES

WALK-
AND-TALK
DATE

This may well be Claudia's all-time favorite Getting-in-Shape Date, as she likes to both walk and talk! Dave is a good listener and needs the exercise too, so several times each week you will find us walking and talking.

THE IDEA:
Over the years we've discovered that our Walk-and-Talk Dates are quite productive. Many times when we are in the middle of writing a chapter or article and we're fresh out of creativity, we are able to get back on track if we walk and talk about it. If walking causes your creative juices to flow, take a tip from us and bring along an index card and pencil. We find if we don't write down all our ideas, we've forgotten them by the time we get home.

LEARN THE BENEFITS:
To be honest, we can't think of any other kind of date that is as good for our health and our communication as our Walk-and-Talk Dates. They're cheap and easy. And they're simple. If you are the spontaneous type, this may just be the date for

you. It requires no planning, unless you have small children and have to arrange for a babysitter. And because you can walk just about anywhere, you can have these dates anytime.

CHOOSE YOUR FAVORITE STOMPING GROUNDS:
Some of our favorite walking places are:

- ◆ Would you believe, around our block? It's approximately ½ mile, so if we walk around the block four times, we will have walked approximately two miles. It's also easy. We don't have to get in the car and drive anywhere.

- ◆ Nature trails and mountain paths. More planning and time are needed, but it's worth it.

- ◆ Shopping malls. Many open early to accommodate local walkers. I (Claudia) enjoy walking in malls more than Dave. He doesn't complain as long as the stores are closed since shopping together is not his favorite activity!

- ◆ Historic areas. Many cities and towns have a historic section. Sometimes you can even find a guidebook. This is a great date for history buffs.

- ◆ Outdoor tracks. We like to walk on a track around a couple of soccer fields. It reminds us of one advantage of the empty nest—no soccer practices! With three sons, we lived through thirteen years of soccer games and practices. It's not that we didn't enjoy those years, but we did pay our dues.

◆ Walking and biking paths. You don't have to watch out for cars—just bikes!

◆ The beach. This is our all-time favorite place to walk.

Add your favorite walking places to our list and get ready for a fun way to stay in shape. This date, while great for your health, will keep your marriage fit too!

BIKE DATE

Bike dates can be as simple as biking around your neighborhood or as elaborate as our friends' Dan and Leah's Great Bike Date, a cross-country foliage biking tour in the hills of Vermont. Here's what Dan and Leah told us:

THE IDEA:

"For our tenth anniversary we decided to take an October bike tour of Vermont. The leaves were incredible. It's amazing how much more dramatic they are when you are out in the open air seeing them than when you see them from inside your car. Our first experience was so exhilarating that we repeated it for our eleventh anniversary."

They skipped last year but tell us they are headed back to Vermont this fall for their third bike tour. That is quite an endorsement, so we asked more questions.

PLAN FOR THE ESSENTIALS:

"Where do you stay at night?" we asked. This was a key question for us, as we used all our camping-out energy when our three sons were growing up.

"Oh," Leah answered, "we stay at quaint little country inns." She immediately had our attention.

"But what about your clothes and baggage?" Claudia asked, being the practical one. We then discovered the tour provides a van to take your luggage from one inn to the next.

"Biking makes me awfully hungry. Where do you eat lunch?" Dave inquired.

Dan cleared up that one. "We receive instructions each morning. They tell us what route to take and where to stop for lunch. It's usually at a little gourmet inn or teahouse. The food is wonderful, and the morning of biking gives you the appetite to appreciate it. Because you're burning so many calories, you don't have to watch what you eat. The tour also tells us what to look for as well as where we will be staying that evening. Everything is taken care of. They provide bikes, helmets, and drinking water. They are even prepared to fix flat tires.

"We have two guides and a support van close by. It is a group tour, but the group is small, and it's fun to meet other couples from around the country. The group is so diverse that we don't spend a lot of time talking about children and, in a way, that's nice."

Leah added that the best part for her was being alone with Dan without their children and not having to worry about preparing meals. She loved being able to talk without interruptions or simply, to be quiet.

FOR MORE INFORMATION:
By this time they really had our interest. We learned there are weeklong tours as well as weekend tours. We also filed away the name of their tour group and will include it for your information:

Vermont Bicycle Tours
614 Monkton Road
Bristol, VT 05443-0711
Telephone: 1-800-245-3868
www.vbt.com

For more information you could write or call:
Vermont Chamber of Commerce
P.O. Box 37
Montpelier, VT 05601
Telephone: 802-223-3443
http://www.vtchamber.com/visiting/index.html

CONSIDER ALTERNATIVES:

We realize this date is one of the supersplurge suggestions. If these trips don't fit your budget or your schedule but you want to bike together, you can plan your own trip, even for a day near your home. You can pack a lunch and rent two bikes and ride through your local park or greenway. It isn't exactly the same as a week of riding in Vermont, but take it from us, it's fun! We know, because we've done it. Maybe next year we can try Vermont!

NEW-SPORT DATE

We'll never forget our most traumatic sports date—our first adventure on snow skis. Recently, we read that the beginning skier needs "adventure in the soul, bravery in the heart, strength in the body—and brakes." When we had our first New-Sport Date, learning to ski, thirty years ago, we qualified for adventure, bravery, and strength—but the "brakes" part was missing!

THE IDEA:

We were living in southern Germany and most everybody skied—or so our friends told us—as they presented us with their old, used skis. Knowing nothing about skiing, we didn't know our gift skis were so ancient that they should have been in a ski museum—not on our feet. Dave was the first to discover they had no brakes, as he not so gracefully fell between two signposts and slid under the sign. We quickly learned that the only way to stop was to fall, sit down, or hit something—or someone.

Our first New-Sport Date obviously was not that successful. But we are adventurous at heart and we did live right in the middle of ski country, so our tenacity won out. After a few lessons and lots of practice, we found we were enjoying skiing more and falling less. We even learned how to "snowplow" and come to a complete stop without hitting another skier.

One thing that motivated us to stick with it was the number of senior citizens we saw on the ski slopes. We felt certain that if they could ski, we should be able to ski. (They also got discounted tickets—something for us to look forward to someday.) Skiing was also a hit with our three sons, who at one time or another all raced competitively.

SAVE YOURSELF SOME PAIN:
If you are even thinking about a ski date as your New-Sport Date, let us save you the pain and suffering we've experienced with the following suggestions.

1. Ski equipment is more important than ski clothes. Start with short skis. Our first skis towered way above our heads and looked more like skis for ski jumping. I (Claudia) wore bright orange, so if I fell or wandered off the beaten path, I could be found. I didn't think about how conspicuous I would look or how self-conscious I would feel on the slopes in my bright orange.

2. Take lessons! Unless you are a kid or are extremely athletic, it will not come naturally. A good ski instructor can help you enjoy this date faster, better, and safer.

3. Don't overdress. We can remember feeling like mummies with all our extra socks, underwear, turtlenecks,

sweaters, jackets, hats, earmuffs, and gloves. No wonder we couldn't get up when we fell. We couldn't even move! On the other hand, our many layers of clothes kept us warm and protected us from bruising too badly when we fell. Look for lightweight, water-resistant ski clothes, like ski jackets and pants made of Gortex and silk underwear. Mittens will keep your hands warm but make it hard for you to maneuver when you need to get a tissue out of your pocket.

4. Don't try to carry a lot of extra stuff with you as you ski. Sure, you may get hungry, but lunch in a fanny pack may be completely squashed by the time you decide to eat it. Basics for us were tissues, lip balm, and some money for when we were hungry.

CONSIDER ALTERNATIVES:

If you are brave enough to choose a ski date as your New-Sport Date, let us encourage you to stick with it. As one person put it, "Skiing is some skill, lots of instinct, hard work, insanity, and practice, practice, practice!"

If other safer sports like tennis, golf, or one-on-one basketball are more appealing to you, that's fine. Choose a sport you both will enjoy learning. You're in for an adventure and a treat. By the way, we've even made it down a few black slopes!

12

SNOW-GOLF DATE

Our only golf experience was in the middle of the summer in Albuquerque, New Mexico. Dave's Aunt Jo gave us a Golf Date to introduce us to her favorite sport. She even included lessons with a local pro.

THE IDEA:
We have more of a spirit of adventure than of athletic ability, but we got into it enough to put golfing on our future list of Sports-to-Pursue Dates. However, I don't know if we will ever be adventurous enough to try winter golf in the snow. Our friends, Bill and Karen, say it's a great date. Here's their report.

TAKE LIFE AT A SNOW PACE:
"Every year we take the time to set goals for the new year and to reflect on our past year together. One January, we hired a sitter to spend the night with our toddler and we took off for an overnight at a local park lodge. It was a beautiful atmosphere. There were few people around as it is basically a summer resort. Our room overlooked a frozen lake and snow-covered golf course.

"That evening we enjoyed a long dinner by candlelight.

The warm, glowing fire in the fireplace added to our pleasure and ability to relax as we talked about our marriage, our goals, our love for each other, and our dreams for our lives.

"The next morning, after a leisurely breakfast, we went out and played a round of winter golf. The whole golf course was ours. We didn't have to wait for a group to finish the next hole. We talked continually, with no interruptions, as we drove around the course in our golf cart looking for our orange golf balls in the white snow. It was truly a date filled with love, and lots of communication."

"Who won?" we asked.

"We didn't really keep score," Bill said, "but we both remember winning!"

If you love risks and like the snow, take Bill and Karen's dating suggestion. It's a round of golf you both can win!

WATER
DATE

THE IDEA:

"The ultimate Water Date" one couple told us, "is to go sailing in the middle of winter." But unless you live in the South Seas and have your own little sailboat, this also may be the ultimate in expensive dates. Several other couples we know share their enthusiasm, so we are including this date for the rich, though maybe not-so-famous.

Our friends, together with two other couples, flew to the eastern Caribbean Islands where they chartered a fifty-foot sailing yacht. This was not your standard sailboat. It came complete with a captain, cook, and three cozy staterooms with private baths. For one week, they sailed around the Virgin Islands.

Our friends swore this was the ultimate date for the workaholic. Think about a week with no phone calls, no television, no contact with your business, no control over things at home. Your only contact with the outside world is the yacht's radio for emergencies! (On this date—even if you have a world cell phone—we suggest leaving it at home!)

REAP THE BENEFITS OF LIMITED SPACE:

We are not great water enthusiasts and have absolutely no experience with sailboats, so we asked, "What did you do for a week on a fifty-foot boat?"

Their faces lit up as they told us how they were forced to relax. They ate gourmet food, helped sail the boat, read, snorkeled, swam, sat around, talked, and laughed with their friends. They also said that the V-shaped berths left them no room not to be intimate.

One note of caution from our friends: it is critical that the other couples you go with are very good friends or this date could backfire. A good economy cruise could provide the same background for togetherness (and the stateroom would be larger).

CONSIDER ALTERNATIVES:

If you are not in the rich-and-famous category, don't rule out a Water Date. We'll never forget the time we went whitewater rafting—the only time! Claudia spent all of her energy watching and waiting in fear of the famous Devil Shoals. Once back on land, we decided to leave this date for those braver than us.

We hear canoeing can be fun and relaxing. Maybe you like to swim or water-ski. Actually, the Water Date that sounds the most interesting to us is a Jacuzzi in a nice hotel. Whatever Water Date you choose, just taking the initiative will make a splash with your mate!

14
DANCING-
LESSONS
DATE

THE IDEA:

One Christmas we splurged and bought a new stereo system. For years we used hand-me-down stereo equipment from our three sons. We've had so much fun listening to our old records and tapes, we wonder why we didn't do this sooner. Talk about musical memories—we've got them! Some of our records go way back to our college days and times of dancing cheek to cheek. (We were in the era of the twist.)

Holidays often bring out the sillies in us, and that Christmas was no exception. We began to show our family how our generation danced. We also showed ourselves that we could benefit from a Dancing-Lessons Date.

TAKE THE FIRST STEP:

Call your local studio. Sounds great, but how do you start? Our friend Michele suggested calling the local dance studios and asking if they had any specials. The studios also usually know if there are any upcoming free dances or charity balls.

"If you attend a charity ball, you may even be able to deduct at least part of the cost of the tickets from your taxes," Michele told us.

One hotel in our city hosts a free monthly tea dance with swing music. Occasionally, local dance studios offer drawings. If you are as lucky as Michele, you may also win a free one-hour dance lesson.

SHAPE UP BY LINE DANCING AND/OR SQUARE DANCING:
Other friends of ours love to square dance and also do line dancing. But let us warn you, we recently went to a square dance and were completely exhausted after a couple of hours. Well, after all, it serves us right. This is a Getting-in-Shape Date! What more can we say?

15
WORKOUT DATE

THE IDEA:

It started with a back injury but led to a fun date. Would you believe that in our late forties we began working out in a fitness gym? Our adult children had a hard time believing their mom was actually pumping iron. But she was, and she has continued her routine for the last two years.

Our Workout Dates actually started several years ago when I (Claudia) injured my back and required several months of therapy. Part of my therapy program was to work out with light weights and do numerous exercises. Not only did this benefit my back, it helped my general physical condition so much that Dave decided (under duress) to join me.

Having lived on the cutting edge of stress and overload for so long, it seemed strange to take the time to work out together. We told ourselves we were doing this for my back and for our health. But we discovered we were also doing it for fun.

TALK TO YOUR PHYSICIAN:

You can approach a Workout Date several ways. Before you begin working out, however, check out any physical fitness program with your family doctor. Let him or her guide you in what is sensible and healthy for you.

FIND A PROGRAM WITHIN YOUR BUDGET:
As you begin, consider your budget and what you can invest in fitness training. There are many health clubs, aerobic programs, and fitness centers. Initially, we went to a therapy center for those who have been previously injured. Our strength trainer, Ed, guided us in what was safe and beneficial for us. Neither of us were into muscle building; we just wanted to stay healthy and have fun in the process, so this was a great introduction to fitness training.

WORK OUT WITH DVDS AND VIDEOS:
Don't overlook workout videos and DVDs. But here's a word of caution: this is not a competitive date! Don't try to outdo each other. Relax, have fun, and enjoy the fringe benefits of more energy and vigor. You may even discover being in shape will enhance your other dates—particularly, the romantic ones! (That's the next part of this book.)

ROMANTIC DATES

16

HONEYMOON-MEMORY DATE

THE IDEA:

Many people tell us that second honeymoons are better than first ones. We tend to agree. Take a few minutes and think back to your own honeymoon. If you are like us, you can probably laugh about it now.

We got married in the middle of our college years, during the Cuban missile crisis. We thought the world was going to blow up before we had a chance to live together. So in two months, with slight apprehension at our hurry but mostly with their blessings, our families helped us plan and pull off a lovely church wedding. We just didn't get around to planning our honeymoon!

BACK ON THE HOOK:

We have always been the spontaneous types. Apart from reservations the first night, we were definitely ad-libbing it with our honeymoon plans. So years later, when others suggested we re-create our honeymoon, we told them, "We're not sure we really want to." Besides, the motel in Gainesville, Georgia, where we spent our wedding night, had been torn down long ago. We thought we were off the hook on this

45

date—that is, until Claudia's mom was in the hospital in Gainesville and we went to see her.

We found ourselves back in the same town at approximately the same time of year as when we were there on our wedding night many years ago. When we were not at the hospital, we were working on this book. So naturally, we began to talk about our own honeymoon. As we talked, we realized that the motel where we were staying was located about the same place where our honeymoon motel had been.

At breakfast that morning, over who knows how many cups of coffee, we reminisced and realized how far we had come in thirty years of marriage. In some small way, we did go back in history. You can do the same. Here are some tips.

CREATE YOUR OWN HONEYMOON:

1. Have a Memory Date to talk once again about your honeymoon. See how far you have come in the months, years, or maybe even decades since your honeymoon.

2. Actually go back and re-create (or improve on) your honeymoon.

3. Plan a completely new and updated honeymoon. We like this suggestion and have decided we would rather go to Austria than Gainesville, Georgia!

4. Be thankful for all you've learned in your marriage and for all the ways you've grown closer to each other.

THREE-WISHES DATE

THE IDEA:

Yes, our friend actually met her husband at the door one evening in a tutu complete with wings, quiver, and three arrows with hearts. "Tonight is your night!" she told him. "I'm your fairy godmother, and I will grant you three wishes!"

Our friend was quite sketchy about what happened next, but the giggle and silly look on her face told us it was a fun, romantic date. While not asking specific details, we did gather some practical suggestions in case you feel like turning into a fairy godmother or fairy godfather.

HEED THE WARNINGS:

It's best to make this a surprise date. But you've also got to be in the mood for this one. Announcing the day or morning before the date that you're set to be the wish-granting fairy may set both of you up for a letdown. Expectations may build too much. Or your day may get out of hand and be one of those awful days that if you were a fairy you'd want to make yourself disappear—much less grant wishes!

One more caution: some may find that granting three unqualified wishes is a little too threatening. What if a mate asks you to do something you don't want to do? If you are worried about this, you can ask your mate for five wishes; then choose the three you feel comfortable granting. You may be able to relax more this way and enjoy bringing pleasure to your mate.

MAKE A LIST OF YOUR WISHES:

Here are a few wish suggestions:

◆ Thirty-minute back rub

◆ Foot massage and pedicure

◆ Bath—gently bathe your mate, as if you were bathing a baby

◆ Shower for two—take a shower together and wash each other's hair

◆ Lie on a blanket outdoors and gaze at the stars together

Our list ends here, but this can be the beginning of your own brand of creativity. This is one date the fairy godparent may enjoy as much as the lucky subject. At any rate, it should add some sparkle to your love life.

KIDNAP
DATE

THE IDEA:

Are you looking for a way to rekindle the flame of romance in your relationship? Why not do the unexpected?

Claudia will never forget the day I (Dave) came in with three red roses and announced we were leaving in thirty minutes. Off I whisked Claudia to a little hotel in the Vienna Woods. (We were living in Vienna at that time.) After Claudia called and confirmed that there really was a sitter with our three boys, she relaxed. Together, we enjoyed a wonderfully intimate two days and two nights alone.

Romance can be alive and well in your marriage too. Why not kidnap your mate? The element of surprise in the Kidnap Date re-creates that feeling you had when you dated before you married. Others have pulled it off. Listen to one wife's account.

PLAN TO TAKE TIME APART:

"We've found in our sixteen years together, our weekend get-aways keep the spark alive and add spice to our life. Plus there's something about getting away together that creates an atmosphere of relaxation. Uninterrupted time to focus on one another, to talk and laugh and love each other, are like marital vitamins.

"We regularly get away one weekend every other month. We swap kids with another family so every other month we have their children for a weekend. For us, it's really worth it. So when I decided to surprise my husband, babysitting was already taken care of.

"I contacted my husband's business and, unknown to him, arranged for him to leave early on Friday afternoon. Others in his office cooperated and covered his appointments and other commitments. I then worked out the children's after-school schedule and rides to the home where they were spending the weekend.

"Friday finally arrived. I felt like a kid again. I packed the car with our clothes, food munchies, favorite music, candles, bubble bath—you get the picture! I then picked up my husband at work, blindfolded him, and led him to the car—the passenger side. I instructed him to lie back and relax while I drove to our mountain hideaway about forty-five minutes away. I previously had reserved a room with our own fireplace and Jacuzzi. Let the fun begin!"

MAKE THE MOST OF THE UNEXPECTED:

"When we arrived, my husband was so excited about our romantic weekend away that he couldn't unload the car fast enough. Now, as much as I'd like to leave the rest of our romantic rendezvous to your imagination, I have to be honest and tell you what happened next.

"As he bent over to set our luggage down, his back went into spasm. Yes, we did spend the weekend in bed, but it wasn't quite as romantic as what we had in mind. However, the weekend is still one of our favorite memories. We had hours and hours just to talk. There were no interruptions. He couldn't move, so there was no place to go.

"We reaffirmed our commitment to one another. How does it go? 'In sickness and in health . . .' We can now add, 'With healthy backs and with hurting backs!'"

Laugh at the Memories—Good and Bad:

The Arps also have had our disappointments—like the time we were staying at a romantic country inn and got locked out. We ended up spending the night in our minivan! But let us encourage you to keep planning and keep surprising each other. Even the times things don't work out as planned, you're left with memories you can laugh about someday. So go on. Take the chance. Kidnap your mate. He or she will be a happy hostage!

AT-HOME ROMANCE DATE

THE IDEA:

"Believe it or not," a mother of two young children told us, "one of our favorite dates is at home."

"You've got to be kidding," we said in unison. But she meant it. "How do you pull it off?" we asked. Here's her secret.

PLAN AHEAD:

"First, I find out what time my husband expects to arrive home. Then I plan ahead, feed the kids, and get them ready for bed.

"I usually have music playing, candles lit, and dinner warming in the oven by the time he walks in the door. I ask him to put the kids to bed while I'm in the bathroom running a hot bubble bath and lighting candles around the tub.

"After he tucks the children in bed and says good night, I lead him to the bedroom, undress him, and bathe him. Then I tell him to soak and relax while I set dinner on a picnic blanket in front of the fireplace in a candlelit room.

"When he comes downstairs in his robe, the phone is set on voice mail so we won't be disturbed. The rest is optional!"

COACH THE CHILDREN:
"But what about the children?" we asked.

"The children have been coached all day that tonight is special for Daddy and Mommy," she said. "I tell them it is very important that they do their part by obeying rules and staying in bed."

CONSIDER ALTERNATIVES:
Now, we must make a date disclaimer. When our sons were little, no way would we have trusted those three to stay in bed. However, if your kids are more cooperative than ours were and you're a brave and adventurous soul, you can go ahead and give this At-Home Romance Date a try. But if, like us, you're not so brave, farm the kids out for the evening. The rest is up to your ingenuity!

20

BED-AND-BREAKFAST DATE

THE IDEA:
Our very first Bed-and-Breakfast Date started with a Christmas present from friends. We received a wonderful bed-and-breakfast guidebook with vivid descriptions of B and Bs around the country. Knowing our empty nest was fast approaching, our friends wanted us to be prepared for a new kind of date. So far, each time we have used their gift, we haven't been disappointed.

Interestingly, some of our favorites aren't the elaborate, expensive ones. We like to stay in places that are a little more austere and have lots of history. They're usually cheaper too!

LOOK FOR SOMEPLACE UNIQUE:
That we at least passed something down to the next generation became obvious when one of our sons and daughter-in-law told us about one of their favorite Bed-and-Breakfast Dates. They went to an old, old hotel in Minnesota called the Anderson House. Its uniqueness? It's the oldest operating hotel in that state, dating back to the 1850s, and is still run by the original family (or at least by their descendants).

They liked the Dutch European influences in the structure of the building. It wasn't your upscale hotel, but it was unusual and eccentric. For instance, it had seventeen house cats guests could rent for the night. This couple loved cats and at the time had two of their own. So they had fun renting a cat for the evening but admitted they felt unfaithful to their own cats, Pete and Sebastian.

We're not sure we would go so far as to rent a cat, but we hear that petting a cat lowers your blood pressure. Perhaps that's what makes the Anderson House such a relaxing place to stay.

CHECK THIS LIST BEFORE YOU GO:

If we have whetted your appetite for a Bed-and-Breakfast Date, consider the following few tips:

1. Make reservations well in advance. We can still hear the owner of one B and B laughing. We called for reservations the day of our trip and discovered they book their rooms years in advance. That's unusual, but it is wise to book accommodations several weeks or months in advance.

2. Ask about their smoking or nonsmoking policy. Most B and Bs are small, and smoke may carry throughout the house. Claudia has an allergy to smoke. Once we stayed in a quaint, old house, but both of the owners and all the other guests smoked. It was not one of our most pleasant experiences.

3. Check the pet policy. Some allow pets, while others

don't. This may affect you even if you don't have pets. We'll long remember one B and B experience. It was not unlike the Anderson cat hotel, but dogs were the pet of choice. The owner had two dogs, and the other guest had two Irish wolfhounds that were about the size of Shetland ponies. There almost wasn't room for us and the rest of the guests.

4. Visit bed-and-breakfasts with a spirit of adventure. You will find that no two are the same. On your Book Date (Date 7) you may want to check out books on bed-and-breakfasts and country inns. We recommend the following:

◆ *The Complete Guide to Bed & Breakfasts, Inns & Guesthouses in the United States, Canada, & Worldwide,* by Pamela Lanier (Lanier Publishing Intl., Ltd., 2002).

◆ *Bed and Breakfasts and Country Inns,* 15th ed., by Deborah Sakach (American Historic Inns, 2003).

◆ In addition, AAA has given us good travel information.

Most helpful of all is the chance to get away together and explore. Choose your own style—from country inns to seaside or mountain lodges, mansions, farmhouses, or ranches. Who knows what adventures lurk just ahead? You may even end up renting your very own cat!

21

SWINGING-
IN-THE-JUNGLE
DATE

THE IDEA:

Do you harbor a secret desire to go on an African safari? Or maybe you dream about a vacation for two on a deserted island, but your budget is a better fit with the dollar theater and popcorn. If so, you may be a candidate for a Swinging-in-the-Jungle Date. Our friends say it's more fun than a barrel of monkeys. Here's how the wife describes this special date.

"The night before our first Jungle Date we sat and stared at our depleted checkbook. The funds weren't there for a major vacation that summer, and we had just made a commitment to let our credit cards collect dust instead of interest. Seeing my husband's disappointment motivated me to come up with an 'at-home' fun getaway date. Thus the origination of our Swinging-in-the-Jungle Date."

BRING HIM/HER HOME WITH A MYSTERIOUS INVITATION:

"First I called my husband and left a message on his voice mail, something like, 'Honey, I'm so glad you chose me as your mate . . . We may not be able to afford an African safari, but let's swing in the jungle tonight. See you later!'"

DRESS FOR THE JUNGLE:

"When he arrived home, I met him at the door in Me Jane attire. (I wore an aerobic workout outfit and leotard skirt.) I then led Tarzan to a picnic dinner set up in our backyard tree house. If you don't have a tree house, improvise with a picnic table and blanket. If the weather is inclement, consider a covered or screened porch. If it's cold, set up your jungle in the den or in front of the fireplace. Add plants all around to resemble a jungle."

KEEP THE FARE SIMPLE:

"I tried to be creative with the picnic food and to carry out the jungle theme with bananas, coconuts, berries, pineapples, nuts, and mangoes. Candles added to the atmosphere, but later we blew them out and watched the moon and stars appear. It wasn't quite like Africa, but it sure beat leftovers!

"The next summer we were able to take a vacation, but tucked in our memory bank of fun experiences are our nights at home swinging in the jungle!"

CLUE
DATE

Surprises run in our family. When one of our sons wanted to really surprise his date, he chartered a small plane to fly them around the Chicago skyline. His date had no idea where they were going. The original plan was to land at an airport in downtown Chicago, go out for dinner and to the theater, and then take a limousine back to the college campus. When he found out how much all of that would cost, this romantic dude realized that even five-star dates have their limit and he stuck with just the plane ride.

THE IDEA:
If your mate likes surprises and enjoys not knowing where you are going or what you are doing, why not have a Clue Date? Give your mate clues—perhaps in poetry or jingles if you are poetic or wish to be—for each part of your special date. Try the following:

LEAVE A CREATIVE TRAIL OF CLUES:
Clue One—This clue might include the invitation and suggestion of attire for the date. You might say something like:

How about a date Friday night at eight?
It will be far from normal, so please dress formal!

Clue Two—Give a hint of where you are going. If you are going to an outdoor concert, you could give this clue:

Music is fun and calms the soul,
But take a coat because it may be cold!

Another place you might consider going is a favorite restaurant. If your budget is tight, go out for dessert or a cup of coffee or tea. Plays, lectures, and movies are also great places to go on Clue Dates.

Clue Three—To top off a romantic evening, you may want to whisk your mate off to a motel with a Jacuzzi or hot tub, or take your mate home and pretend your bathroom is a spa. For this part of the evening, you could give this clue:

Rub a dub dub, two lovers in a tub!

We suggest following your "water adventure" with an extensive back rub by candlelight. For a warm, romantic feeling, use lotion you've warmed in the microwave.

CONSIDER ALTERNATIVES:
Another type of Clue Date your mate will appreciate is a special letter sent in advance, complete with clues, inviting

him or her for a date. Include the time to be ready for your date and what to wear. For example, you may want to suggest wearing warm-ups and surprise your mate with a romantic walk at night!

Surprise dates can be elaborate or simple, expensive or cheap, long or short. They can add fun, excitement, and adventure to your dating life. They are great rut-removers and can be the spark to add romance to your relationship. Give it a try. You may be surprised at the results!

DO-IT-
TOGETHER
DATES

23
HOME-
IMPROVEMENT
DATE

THE IDEA:

From time to time we have dreamed of restoring an old house. Our dreams, however, always include the wherewithal to do it. If we had to do the work ourselves, it would be a nightmare. We're not that handy, but our next generation is more talented.

We realized this when one of our sons and his wife bought their first house, an old English Tudor built in 1931. We were able to combine a speaking engagement with a visit with them in their "new" old home, so we offered to be their slaves for several days.

It was actually fun to scrub, clean, hang wallpaper, unpack boxes, and be their helpers. It also brought back memories of our eleven moves, which have spanned several continents, as well as memories of all of our Home-Improvement Dates!

Wallpapering Dates are probably our favorite Home-Improvement Dates. It may take two to tango, but for us it definitely takes two to wallpaper. We have our system down. I (Dave) apply the paste. Claudia hangs the paper. And we both feel proud when it stays on the wall!

BEWARE OF THE HAZARDS:
Once, when we were living in Vienna, we wallpapered our whole apartment. Our bedroom was the last room, and we were running low on wallpaper paste. No problem; we simply thinned it. That was in the summer. That winter when the heat came on and the walls adjusted to the change of climate, our wallpaper decided to adjust too. In the middle of one night, we heard a rustling sound. We turned on the light just in time to see our wallpaper peeling off the wall in large strips. The next day we had another Wallpaper Date to re-hang it!

MAKE A TO-DO LIST:
What projects would you love to get accomplished around your house? Why not make a list? Then check your latent talents and resources. Some couples love to paint together. We know one couple who painted the outside of their house. Maybe you really want to clean out and organize the basement. Tackle it together.

LOOK FOR WAYS TO LEARN THE SKILLS YOU LACK:
If you're worried about your home-improvement skills, or lack thereof, take heart, you can learn to do anything from repairing cracks in plaster walls to hanging blinds and wallpaper. You can sign up for classes at your local home-improvement store.

Another option is to buy or rent an instructional DVD or video from your video store. Also, some home-improvement stores have videos for loan. This could even be another date—to watch home-improvement videos and choose your home-improvement project. Or you may even decide to take a class. Not only will your home be improved, but you may enjoy the process.

24

STUDY DATE

THE IDEA:

We've decided that learning keeps you young and keeps your life from stagnating. So our next Do-It-Together Date suggestion is to take a class together.

Adult educational opportunities abound, especially if you live in a town with a college or university. You can find classes offered in everything from aerobics to art appreciation. Your local YMCA/YWCA also offers many kinds of classes to get involved in.

CONSIDER THE POSSIBILITIES:

Consider taking classes or lessons in one or more of the following areas:

music appreciation	art history
ceramics and pottery	art
financial management	voice
Bible/religion/theology	aerobics
foreign language	massage
music (One couple we know recently learned to play the guitar.)	

Add the skills you've dreamed of learning about to our list, and choose something you'd like to learn together. We chose a foreign language, but it was under duress and out of need.

CONSIDER THE BENEFITS:
We were living in Vienna and were doing okay with our German in day-to-day living. But to be really effective, we needed to be able to lead marriage workshops in the German language. This required a big (actually a huge) step up from our present level of speaking German, so we decided to jump-start our language study by taking a class together.

The class only lasted a couple of months, so we weren't overwhelmed. We had a goal we could manage; we knew there was a starting point and a finish line.

For some reason language learning is easier for Dave (maybe because he lived in Austria as a young boy), so I (Claudia) needed all the encouragement Dave could give me. We found it was fun to study together—especially after class in a small Viennese coffee shop.

There were other benefits. We met interesting people in the class, including a high government official from France and an American girl with whom we still keep in touch. It was a rewarding experience for us, so it's easy to suggest that you choose your own field of study and enjoy a Study-Together Date with your mate.

25

REMEMBER-WHEN DATE

THE IDEA:

Face it. Some things just have to get done. Why not turn some of the mundane chores of life into a fun date? Most any job is more enjoyable when you tackle it together. It helps, too, if you can make a game out of it. We suggest you try remembering when.

Back in ages past—before you were married—remember how much you looked forward to doing routine chores together? We remember finding our little terrace apartment (others would have called it a basement apartment) and how much we looked forward to living there together. As we stood in the small kitchen, we couldn't wait to share the joy of washing and drying our very own dishes. Even making up our bed and cleaning the bathroom sounded romantic then. My, how things change!

If things have changed at your house too, if you're under the pile and need a united front to get back on top, consider turning your chores into a Remember-When Date. As you do routine chores together, remember when you dreamed about doing these things together—before you were married.

Take a Refreshing Step Back in Time:
Recently, we were in Atlanta, Georgia, and decided to see if we could still remember how to get to our first apartment. We actually did find it and sat in our car and remembered.

"Remember when we spent a whole day picking out our china and crystal and registering at the local department store?" If you haven't used your good dishes for a long time, perhaps you need to plan a special At-Home Dinner-for-Two Date.

"Remember when we received our first wedding gift?" As you dust knickknacks, try to remember who gave them to you or on what special occasion you acquired them.

"Remember when we used to go to the Laundromat to wash our clothes?" When our clothes were all dirty, we would feel the urge to spend a weekend with Claudia's parents. They had a great washer and dryer and lived only eighty miles away!

Consider the Alternatives:
A variation of the Remember-When Date is to grocery shop together. As you go up and down the aisles, remember the first times you grocery shopped together. We remember having an argument over angel food cake. Dave picked up an angel food cake mix. Claudia was insulted that he thought she couldn't make one from scratch. (Now we simply buy one from the bakery.) Notice items you used to purchase that you no longer need. We zip right by the baby food section, animal crackers, and Gatorade!

REMEMBER IN SILENCE:

If you prefer working together in silence, you may want to make a mental list of your own Remember-Whens. Then, at the end of the day, share a pizza and your lists with each other. Just remembering when working together was such fun may encourage you to tackle your present to-do list as a team.

26
MARRIAGE-
ENRICHMENT
DATE

THE IDEA:
If you have never participated in a marriage education seminar or workshop, or taken a marriage enrichment course, we highly recommend this date. Your own marriage relationship will be enriched by learning some skills and by meeting other couples who are also committed to making their marriages grow.

KEEPING YOUR MARRIAGE ALIVE:
A couple we met in the early eighties, David and Vera Mace, greatly challenged us to work at keeping our marriage alive and were mentors to us over the years in our work as marriage educators. The Maces pioneered marriage enrichment in this country. They believed couples, before they got to the point of needing marriage counseling, could learn skills to make their marriages better. They focused on problem prevention, growth, and potential. They taught couples how to communicate effectively, to deal creatively with anger, to negotiate differences, and to express appreciation. In 1973, on their fortieth wedding anniversary, the Maces founded the Association of Couples in Marriage

73

Enrichment (ACME) an international network of couples working for better marriages.

We met the Maces when we attended one of their training workshops, and we were intrigued by this couple who were in their late seventies and still had a vibrant, loving, and alive marriage, a commitment they had kept for fifty years. We returned for the advanced training, also led by the Maces, and over the years they have had substantial input in our lives. One great privilege for us was coauthoring with Vera one of the Occasional Papers for the 1994 United Nations International Year of the Family.

SEMINAR SUGGESTIONS:
Today there are many excellent marriage education courses, seminars, and workshops to choose from. For an extensive listing see www.smartmarriages.com. You can also subscribe to the free SmartMarriages e-mail newsletter and receive the latest marriage education news and updates.

Realizing that we cannot list all of the great resources, we do suggest the following national programs:

- ◆ Prevention and Relationship Enhancement Program (PREP) — www.prepinc.com

- ◆ Marriage Alive Seminar — www.marriagealive.com

- ◆ Life Innovations — www.lifeinnovations.com

- Couple Communication —
  www.couplecommunication.com

- Association for Couples in Marriage
  Enrichment (ACME) — www.bettermarriages.org

- Les and Leslie Parrott —
  www.realrelationships.com

- Family Life Conference — www.familylife.com

- Smalley Relationship Center —
  www.smalleyonline.com

- Michelle Weiner-Davis — www.divorcebusting.com

- SmartMarriages Annual International
  Conference — www.smartmarriages.com

GET A MARRIAGE COACH:
Another way to get smart about your marriage is to hire a marriage coach. A few sessions with a marital coach can help you set goals for your future and be more intentional about your marriage. Here are three coaching resources to get you started:

Natelle and Curt Brown — www.matchkeepers.com
Christopher McCluskey — www.christianliving.com
Doug McKinley — www.madaboutyou.org

27
HOST-A-
DINNER-PARTY
DATE

THE IDEA:

We aren't gourmet cooks, but a couple of Dinner-Party Dates we've pulled off stand out in our memory banks as super fun.

**GIVE A FRIEND FROM ANOTHER COUNTRY
A TASTE OF AMERICAN TRADITION:**

The first was a Valentine dinner party we gave for our German friends years ago when we were living in Germany. Valentine's Day originated in Italy, but we have adopted the holiday into our American traditions. At that time Valentine's Day was seldom celebrated in Germany, so we decided to give our German friends a little taste of America.

What made this dinner party so much fun was an offer by our good friends, Clark and Ann, to be our servants for the evening. Their German was better than ours, which helped the after-dinner conversation. Our friends especially liked the cherry pie and our stories about George Washington and the cherry tree. (We included a little American history in our celebration.)

INVITE A SPECIAL GUEST OR SPEAKER:

Our other favorite Dinner-Party Date was in Vienna when we hosted a dinner in our home for our Austrian friends. Our guests of honor were Stan and Maggie Smith. Tennis fans will recognize Stan Smith as one of the world's tennis greats. He was in Vienna playing in a tennis tournament and graciously agreed to come share about his tennis and personal life with our friends. We met the Smiths through mutual friends, also living in Vienna. They not only cohosted the dinner with us, they provided a caterer to do all the work! Now you know why it was such a favorite date.

PLAN A PLANNING DATE:

If funds for catering aren't there and you don't have friends willing to be your servants, don't discard this date suggestion. Our friends Janie and John assure us it's fun to pull it off on your own. Janie tells us about it.

"Don't let the idea of hosting a dinner party scare you. It may be more fun than work—especially if you tackle it as an extended date with your mate. We've had so much fun that we've organized a monthly gourmet club with two other couples and alternate between our three homes. John has even discovered a new hobby—cooking! This makes it all the more enjoyable. We now have a whole string of dates for each dinner party.

"Our initial date is to plan the menu. We enjoy thumbing through gourmet magazines and special-occasion cookbooks. John usually chooses the entrée since he cooks that part of the meal. Together we decide what side dishes and appetizers complement the meal. I like to choose the dessert for the evening. After planning the menu, we compile our shopping list.

"On our second date we grocery shop together. We like to go to a local grocery store that offers samples and gourmet coffee to their shoppers.

"The next evening, we decide how the meal will be served. For example, will it be formal or informal, inside or outside? Will we use our good china or everyday dishes?

"The night before our dinner party is the Food-Preparation Date. Whatever we can get done ahead of time we do, from chopping vegetables to making sauces to baking bread. It helps us to put on our favorite CD. This is also the time we give the house a once-over—at least the areas we are using for our dinner party.

"One of the ideas behind our Predinner-Party Dates is to be prepared so we can enjoy the evening with our guests. We try to be dressed and completely prepared at least an hour before our guests arrive. That gives us time for a last-minute check and then time to sit down, relax, and have hors d'oeuvres together. When our doorbell rings, we are ready to greet our guests with a warm welcome and to give them an evening of fun, good food, and relaxation."

One more tip from Janie and John is to keep tabs of the grocery bill. Because their gourmet club is a regular monthly affair, the three couples divide the cost of each meal. They say it's much cheaper than going out to a nice restaurant. The only down side is you do have to wash the dishes and clean up, but it still sounds like a fun date to us.

The atmosphere is more relaxing because there are no time limitations and no other customers waiting for your table.

CONSIDER ALTERNATIVES:

Here's one final tip. If you are like us and your time and creativity are limited, but you still want to host a dinner party, we suggest letting Julia Child help you. Check out *Julia's Kitchen Wisdom: Essential Techniques and Recipes from a Lifetime of Cooking* (Knopf, 2000) for some recipe ideas. It will help you make your Dinner-Party Date as delightful for you as it is for your guests!

28

MARRIAGE-HISTORY DATE

THE IDEA:

If you've been married longer than twenty-four hours, you have a marriage history. If you've been married longer than twenty-four years, you may have forgotten your marriage history! For the latter, this date will help you remember. For the former, it will help you not forget your good times together.

What is a Marriage-History Date? It's anything you choose to do to catalog your good times together; from writing a marriage journal to producing your own video.

Over the years we've had several dates that helped us catalog our marriage history. We love pictures, so we have trays of slides and boxes of snapshots. Before the days of video cameras, we put together our own family slide shows, complete with a soundtrack. A tip: old slides, home movies, and videos can be transferred to DVD, so they can continue to be a fun way to relive your marriage history.

GET OUT THE SLIDES:

One slide show Claudia and our sons made as a surprise for Dave is especially meaningful to us. It starts with our dating days and follows with the birth and history of each son. We knew our sons were serious about a girl when they pulled out this slide show and revealed what our family was really like. It's only been shown to three girls, and all three are now our daughters-in-law!

MAKE A SCRAPBOOK:
One couple we know have a date each year to make a scrapbook of their history for the past twelve months. They include photos, napkins, hotel receipts—whatever conjures up happy memories.

PRODUCE A VIDEO:
Another pair have a standing video date. Every year they plan a special date for their anniversary. Their date includes a candlelight dinner and their video camera. Over dinner they discuss the major events of the last year and jot down their thoughts. After dinner, with their video camera on a tripod, they record their own marriage history for the past twelve months.

Our friends are the organized type. They have edited all their anniversary videos together on one tape and recently transferred them to DVDs. Do they really watch them? Here's what they said.

"Yes we do, and it's bunches of fun. It's amazing to see the difference in our lives from year to year. Not only do we change in our appearance (a few extra pounds here and there, different hairstyles, different clothes), but even more interesting is to see how we have matured and grown closer to each other.

"We've been working on our marriage for eleven years. With so much history behind us, we're going to keep at it."

INCLUDE THE ESSENTIALS:
If you want to video your own marriage history, here are some suggestions of things to include:

◆ Year, month, and day and what you are celebrating (anniversary, birthday, promotion, or a move to a new location)

◆ Major happenings of the last year (If you are just starting this dating tradition, you may want to include a brief summary of your life together, including where you have lived and special things you have done together.)

◆ Humorous happenings

◆ Things you are looking forward to this next year

Whether you collect photos, make videos, DVDs, or write marriage-history books, you'll enjoy this date for years to come. Think of all the good times together you'll someday be able to remember!

29

HOME DEPOT
DATE

THE IDEA:

Where was Home Depot when we needed it years ago?

As we have already indicated, we're not too handy around the house, but establishments like Home Depot, which sell hardware and home decorations, are making it easier for people like us. We appreciate the good advice and tips the staff give happily and at no extra cost. We became well-acquainted with Home Depot the year we did some empty-nest remodeling. But we never considered going there as a date until our friend Pamela told us that her favorite date with her husband, Evans, was to go to Home Depot.

TRY OUT PAMELA'S IDEA:

"You mean," we questioned, "you actually plan a date to go to Home Depot when you don't need anything?" Pamela convinced us the trip could be a relaxing, inexpensive, and fun evening.

"Recently Evans and I bought our first house. It's a fixer-upper, and for us it's a long-term project. We do projects as we have the time and money. Since right now both seem evasive, we enjoy dreaming and getting ideas for future improvements. For us, this makes for a great date."

It took us a while to adjust our thinking and put Home Depot and dating in the same category. We asked Pamela for more details. "If you're not there out of the need to fix something specific, what do you do?"

She assured us it is fun just to go up and down the aisles and talk about what you would like to do in the future. "Also," she added, "you can get great ideas from their kitchen and bath displays."

We began to see her point, so we tried her date suggestion. Claudia loved the garden windows and knows just the place for one in our kitchen. Dave was fascinated with the mirror tiles.

Pamela suggested writing down your ideas and putting them in a file for future reference. She also suggested topping off your date with eating dinner out or catching a movie.

If you pursue this date, here's a tip from the Arps. Watch out for impulse buying. Dave had to return the mirror tiles!

30

MARRIAGE-CHECKUP DATE

THE IDEA:

We suggest that every couple, no matter how long they've been married, have an annual Marriage-Checkup Date. It can be a growing and enriching experience.

GET WHAT YOU NEED TO GET STARTED:

All that is needed for this date are two pens, some paper, and time alone together. Plan for a couple of hours of peace and quiet. Better still, if possible, go away overnight. This may be a great date to combine with a Bed-and-Breakfast Date.

Start by answering the following questions. You may want to write out your answers separately and then discuss them together.

1. What do I like most about my mate? (For instance, Claudia would have to say Dave's easygoing personality and listening ear.)

The thing I like most about my mate is:

_____

2. What was the best thing that happened to us as a couple in the last twelve months? (Dave might say, the time we spent alone together in New England and setting fresh goals for our marriage.)

The best thing that happened to us as a couple in the last twelve months was:

_____

3. If my mate had the power to change one thing about me, what do I think he or she would change? (Claudia is sure Dave would say that she should be neater— especially with the horizontal files on her desk.)

The one thing I think my mate would like to change about me is:

_____

4. Write down five things you'd like to do together with your mate in the next year. (Dave's list might include getting our home office organized and getting away for a week alone in the mountains. Claudia would be sure to include writing a new book and continuing to exercise together.)

Five things I would like to do in the next year with my mate are:

a. _____

b. _____

c. _____

d. _____

e. _____

SET GOALS TOGETHER:

As you enjoy reflecting on the past twelve months of your marriage, set goals for the next twelve months. Combine your list of things you would like to do together and set priorities. Pick a time and place to do your number-one priority. During the next twelve months, work your way through as much of your combined list as possible. This may be one annual checkup you'll look forward to!

CHEAP-AND-EASY DATES

31
GAME
DATE

Have you noticed a subtle shift in our culture? Perhaps we are still feeling the impact of 9/11. Perhaps we realize in a deeper way how important relationships are. From our observations over the past few years, there seems to be a desire to get back to the basics, to slow down the pace, and to return to a simpler lifestyle. A Game Date can help us do just that.

THE IDEA:

Not long ago, when we were in Wisconsin, friends took us to a quaint shopping mall for breakfast. As we were leaving, a man drove up in his horse and buggy. *My,* we thought, *they even have tourist rides here, but who would want to ride a horse and buggy in the snow?*

As we watched the man tie his horse to a pole in the parking lot and then place a blanket on the back of his horse, we began to realize he wasn't there to drive tourists around. We were in Amish country and he was for real. We assume his buggy didn't come with heating or air-conditioning. While we want a simpler life, we don't want to go that far! But we are willing to start the process with a Cheap-and-Easy Game Date.

CHOOSE YOUR FAVORITE GAME:

Actually, this is a fun date from our past. It was just what we could afford when our boys were little and our finances were limited. We needed something cheap, but also easy, so we began our Backgammon Dates. After we got our tribe in bed, we would pull out our backgammon game and go at it. We don't remember who usually won, but we do remember it as being fun and definitely cheap!

One couple we know enjoys popping popcorn and putting together jigsaw puzzles. That's not for us. Claudia would love it, but I (Dave) think puzzles are a total waste of time. One of our worst arguments was over putting together a puzzle. For Claudia, it was relaxing and she wanted me to help her. I found it totally frustrating and definitely not relaxing. I still don't understand why any sane person would spend hours and hours hunting for little pieces that don't fit. We finally compromised by only putting puzzles together on vacations and one at Christmas.

PLAN A SHOP DATE:

What is your favorite game? Checkers? Chess? Trivial Pursuit? Double Solitaire? Scrabble? If you're not sure, why not plan a date to shop for a game? It may be an investment in many fun future dates.

Ask your friends what their favorite games are. You may get some good suggestions. We never got into video games, but others seem to enjoy them. One couple even created their own computer game.

If your nest is empty, look through all those shelves filled with things your kids left behind in their rooms and see what games you can find. I bet we could even find our backgammon set. Who knows? We may revive this Cheap-and-Easy Date, but you can be sure we will let the boxes of puzzles continue to collect dust.

32

MUSIC DATE

THE IDEA:

One thing we loved about living in Vienna was the beautiful music. And we were amazed that much of it was free! Our favorite Music Date was going to Stadt Park, a lovely park near the Opera in downtown Vienna. Not only was the music gratis, but it was accompanied by professional dancers performing Viennese waltzes.

Often as we walked through the streets of Vienna or Salzburg, musicians performed for anyone who would stop and listen. In Austria free music abounded, but once we moved back to the States, we had to look for it. And we finally did. So can you.

LOOK FOR COMMUNITY CONCERTS:

In our hometown we have free concerts from time to time at a downtown park. Occasionally, the city symphony gives free performances. Other concerts are quite inexpensive.

Keep your ears and eyes open for new artists. You may be among the first to hear a future great. We went to an expensive club for dinner one evening and heard Garth Brooks perform before an audience of forty people, so when he first made it, we were among the few who actually knew who he was.

You can also check your local newspaper for free music recitals. If you live near a college or university with a good music department, check with them for a listing of free or inexpensive recitals and concerts. Another source of free concerts is local churches. Our church has several concerts with a full orchestra each year.

WATCH FOR SPECIAL WEEKEND EVENTS:
Local eating establishments may offer live music, especially on the weekends. A Cheap-and-Easy tip from one couple is to order only appetizers or desserts. You can enjoy the entertainment, but your bill won't be exorbitant.

MAKE A DATE TO SHOP FOR MUSIC:
For a Music Date with future benefits, make a date to shop for a new CD. If your budget is really tight, go to a bookstore that sells used CDs. (You may have to use willpower to buy just one, but remember this is a Cheap Date.) Then return home, make a pot of tea, cuddle on the couch, and let the music fill the room. You never know where this date may take you!

WINDOW-
SHOPPING
DATE

THE IDEA:
Window-Shopping Dates are really inexpensive, especially if you go when the stores are closed! And they are even more fun if the one who likes window shopping the least initiates it. Or so says our friend Karen.

MAKE IT A SURPRISE:
"We have a home-based business. With two small children, things can get pretty hectic and tense. We don't have regular help in our office, but on this particular day my husband, Bill, had scheduled someone to help him. They worked diligently in the office all morning.

"As I began to prepare lunch for us and our two preschoolers, in walked Bill's helper. 'I'll finish that,' she said. Imagine my surprise when I looked up and saw my husband standing at the door with my coat in hand, waiting for me.

"What really excited me was the fact that he had planned (no twisted arm) to take me on my favorite free adventure date—window shopping! Also, he had figured out the babysitting (our office helper), and I didn't have to spend hours getting ready. All I had to do was put on my coat!

"First, we went to the dollar matinee at our local theater. Then, over lunch we talked and talked. Next, we hit the shopping malls to window shop. It was inexpensive because we didn't go into any of the stores. We just enjoyed looking."

I (Dave) can empathize with Bill who is not an "inside the store shopper," but occasionally I'm willing to go window shopping with Claudia. For us to make sure this is a Cheap-and-Easy Date, we even go when the stores are closed. We don't always have Bill and Karen's willpower!

CONSIDER THE ADDED BENEFITS:

Here's another twist. As you window shop, pick out all the things you already have that you see in the store windows. Most of us have more than we realize. Be thankful for the abundance of blessings you have and the opportunity to have a Cheap-and-Easy Date.

34

MATE-APPRECIATION DATE

THE IDEA:

According to a recent study, the three top things Americans value are faith in God, good health, and family relationships. Surprisingly, material possessions and accumulation of wealth are way down on the list. This tells us that people are looking for ways to enrich their relationships. Yet, we are often still more kind and show more appreciation to perfect strangers than we do toward our mates. We can't remember being rude to a clerk in a store or to a grocery bagger, yet it's so easy to slip and say unkind things to our mates.

To combat that tendency and to enhance your intimacy, we suggest the following Mate-Appreciation Date.

TAKE TIME TO PREPARE BEFORE THE DATE:

Before your date, take time to answer the following questions.

◆ What personal traits are special to you about your mate? (For example, Dave might list Claudia's creativity, endless energy and enthusiasm, and wisdom.)

My mate's traits that are special to me are:

_____

_____

◆ What has your mate done lately that you especially like? (When Claudia was trying to meet a critical writing deadline, Dave surprised her with her favorite take-out Chinese food.)

I especially appreciated it when my mate:

_____

_____

◆ What do you particularly enjoy doing together? (Claudia might list traveling together.)

The thing I enjoy doing most with my mate is:

_____

_____

Why not go to your favorite park or restaurant and share your list with each other? It takes no money to affirm your mate, but the benefits are something money can't buy!

35
PARADE
OF HOMES
DATE

THE IDEA:
Many cities across the United States have an annual Parade of Homes that features the latest in home design for the eager viewers and prospective home buyers.

We're not in the market for a new home, but we do have a standing date to go to the Parade of Homes each year. It's fun to look at all the updated kitchens and bathrooms and observe all the current home-building trends.

JUST PRETEND:
You can have fun imagining what your life would be like if you lived in different homes in the parade. One year all of the homes were small starters. We had fun thinking back and fantasizing. "How would we like each house if we were just starting out?"

The year we were helping our own home go through the "change of life"—that time when everything wears out—we got great ideas and leads on who is the best and cheapest at various remodeling tasks. (Warning: This date is initially cheap, but it has the potential to require future funding.)

The fantasy turns back to reality when you get the facts

sheet provided at most of the homes. This sheet includes information about the house, such as the square footage, room dimensions, mortgage information, and estimated monthly payments. After reading these every year, we return home and look around at our house and are thankful for what we have.

WATCH THE PAPERS:
Check out your own area. If you don't have a Parade of Homes, watch the papers for open houses. It's a great way to pick up new ideas and a fun way to date your mate!

36
SWITCH DATE

THE IDEA:
This did not start out as a date. It started out as a frustrating drive to church!

BE WILLING TO MAKE FUN FROM FRUSTRATION:
Dave couldn't find his billfold with his driver's license, so I (Claudia) had to drive. I must tell you that driving is not my favorite activity. I assume if we are going somewhere together, Dave will drive.

After church I wasn't quite as irritated, so I opened the car door for Dave and gave him the royal treatment. Instead of driving him home, I took him out for lunch. Of course, I had to pay because he had neither money nor a driver's license.

By then we were really into our roles, and for the rest of the day, we played "switch." (By the way, he found his billfold. It was with the glasses he had also misplaced.)

KEEP IT SIMPLE:
Years ago, when men typically planned and paid for everything, Switch Dates were called TWIRPP Dates. TWIRPP stood for "the woman is responsible for planning and paying." To simplify the Switch Date, just switch what you typi-

cally do. If your mate usually brings in the paper, you get it. Whoever usually cooks breakfast gets to be served.

Sit in each other's place at the dinner table. If you have children, they may enjoy participating in this dinnertime shuffle. Let each person act like the person in whose place he is sitting. This can be quite revealing. No one—absolutely no one—can imitate parents as well as their own son or daughter!

One benefit of a Switch Date is that it helps you to be more aware of who does what, and it may alert you if one of you should be more involved in helping out the other.

37

SLUMBER-PARTY DATE

THE IDEA:

If you are looking for Cheap and Easy Dates, there's a good chance you have friends who are too. One couple who fits this description told us about their Slumber-Party Date. For us it brought back some fond memories.

We were off on a ski retreat with a group of families and were staying in an old Swiss hotel with high ceilings and squeaking floors. Our youngest son was too young to ski, so we took turns skiing. Dave went skiing with our other two sons in the morning, and Claudia skied with them in the afternoon. After the boys skied all day, they ice-skated in the early evening; so they fell quickly asleep after they got ready for bed.

BE SPONTANEOUS:

One particular evening, another couple put their equally tired kids to bed and came down to our room. We talked and laughed into the wee hours of the night. Finally, we told our friends good night and they went back down the hall to their room.

A few minutes later, as we were getting ready for bed,

there was a knock on our door. Who should appear but our friends? Their two children had locked them out of the room. Try as hard as they could, they were unable to wake up their kids. So we had a Slumber-Party Date. We made a makeshift bed on our floor for our friends, and they spent the night with us.

OR PLAN TO MAKE IT HAPPEN:
We didn't anticipate our Slumber-Party Date, but other friends planned theirs. Here's what they told us.

"Our Slumber-Party Date included two other couples and us. We are all close, longtime friends. All of us were broke and looking for something fun and outrageous to do, so we decided to have a slumber party.

"Everybody brought his own sleeping bag, favorite video or DVD movie, bottle of pop, and junk food. We moved our furniture out of the way and had an all-night flick party. When people got tired, they went to sleep. It reminded us of being back in high school and going to youth retreats. The next day we had to return to our adult world, but for one night we had a great party!"

It did sound like fun, but we're not sure our backs would make it through the night. We prefer slumber parties for two, but if it rings your bell, plan your own Slumber-Party Date. After an all-night party, you'll be all ready for the next part of our fifty-two dates—the "We're Just Too Tired" Dates.

"WE'RE JUST TOO TIRED" DATES

38

PLAY-WITH-A-PET
DATE

THE IDEA:

When we get too old and feeble to travel, we're going to get a pet. In the meantime, we enjoy being around the menagerie of cats that belongs to our sons and their families. At one time they had five cats!

We remember thinking, "What would a young couple in graduate school want with three cats?" From observing our own family zoo, we think we know the answer. It makes for inexpensive entertainment—especially when you're too tired to do anything else. Their three feline friends add fun to life.

REGAIN EMOTIONAL HEALTH:

If you are just too tired for the more strenuous dates, you can sit around and play with your animals. Psychologists tell us pets can be therapeutic and good for our emotional health.

When we were first married, we did have a pet—a hamster named Basel. You may not believe this, but Basel was a wedding present! (Claudia's brother has a funny sense of humor.) We did enjoy our pet, but Basel was a problem hamster. He kept breaking out of his cage and chewing the fringe off our chenille bedspreads. (Remember those?)

CONSIDER ALTERNATIVES:

If you, like us at present, have no furry friends, don't despair. You can still have a Play-with-a-Pet Date. Here are three suggestions:

1. Visit a pet store. One pet store in our town lets the cats that are for sale roam the store. Customers can pet and visit with the cat of their choice.

2. Offer to "sit" your neighbor's pet for an evening. When our boys were growing up, we used to pet-sit long enough to know who really had to take care of them — and it wasn't our three boys! But a pet for an evening can be fun.

3. Check the phone book for the number of your local animal shelter, Society for the Prevention of Cruelty to Animals (SPCA), or Humane Society. We hear that some animal shelters like for people to come walk the dogs and play with the cats. If this is true in your town, don't rule this out as a fun date when you're too tired to talk to people.

Disclaimer: We assume no responsibility for any pet purchases or adoptions resulting from this date!

39

SECRET TLC
DATE

THE IDEA:

Working together has its frustrations. Working together at home simply adds to them! Many entrepreneurial couples are now working together out of their homes. We have done this for years and are always looking for tips to survive the pressure of home and business being in the same location. Our friend, Karen, offered a great tip. When the pressure begins to build, slip off and have a Secret-Closet Date.

LOOK FOR A CHANCE TO SNEAK IN SOME TLC:

"Our secret, spur-of-the-moment date," Karen shared, "is in our walk-in closet. We slip into our closet and close the door. It's one place we can get away, at least briefly, from our three noisy preschoolers. Our Closet Dates usually last only a few minutes, but hiding from the kids makes it fun and 'forbidden.' Although we do try to go out on dates, these Closet Dates are inexpensive, convenient, and sneaky. They also give us a large dose of TLC that we both need to get through the day."

You may have to have a Work-Together Date of cleaning out the closet before you try this date. If you don't have a walk-in closet, or the time to clean it, try the bathroom.

FIND A SECRET PLACE AT THE OFFICE:

Here's a suggestion from Julie for a Secret TLC Date for couples who work outside the home.

"Our offices aren't that far apart, so we ride to work together and park our car about halfway between our two offices. We sometimes plan to take our morning or afternoon break at the same time and meet in the parking lot. What do we do? We park ourselves in our car and snuggle and talk. The time is usually hurried and limited, but it gives us that shot in the arm we need to get through our day."

Take these suggestions or come up with your own Secret TLC Dates. They will help you overcome that feeling of being just too tired.

BLAND DATE

THE IDEA:

There are times we are all under the weather, but dating in that condition isn't much fun unless you are Brenda and Mike. (You may remember them as the Blue-Highways Daters, Date 8.)

Brenda and Mike had both been under a lot of stress. And the stress increased when they discovered one of them had an ulcer. So what did this most unusual couple do? First, they had to slow down. They also had to change their diet, and that's how they came up with this unique date. Since one of them had to eat bland food, they decided to have a Bland Date.

PLAN TO KEEP IT PLAIN:

What do you do on a Bland Date?

"First," Brenda and Mike told a friend of ours, "we wore bland clothes, and what is more bland than beige? Beige matched our bummed-out feeling.

"Next, we listened to old, bland, and very low-key music, like Andy Williams, the Lettermen, and the Carpenters. And we concluded the evening with a slide show of a trip Mike took with his family to Carlsbad Caverns and Los Angeles, when he was fourteen."

What did they eat on this date? The blandest food they could find—chicken, white rice, baked apples, and vanilla ice cream. Their mild, colorless menu blended perfectly with their clothing!

Our hats off to Brenda and Mike. We're smart enough to know having a bland date didn't make their ulcer go away, but they proved you can have a fun date even when you don't feel like it. They leave us no room to say, "We're just too sick and tired to date our mate!"

41

"WE'RE JUST TOO TIRED TO TALK" DATE

THE IDEA:

Sometimes we are just too tired to talk—or should we say sometimes I (Dave) am too tired to talk. Claudia can always talk. But recently, even Claudia was talked out.

We had just returned from leading Marriage Alive workshops back-to-back in several different cities, and even we were tired of talking about marriage. We didn't want to see people or do anything that required any energy at all, so we had a "We're Just Too Tired to Talk" Date. This date required no energy because we prepared for it beforehand.

BE READY TO BE TIRED:

We don't watch a lot of television, but when we are out of town or busy and know we're going to miss a good program or movie, we try to record it so we can watch it when we are home. The problem is we usually never get around to watching the shows we've recorded. You see, we have this bad habit of not labeling the tape or DVD we use, and then we record over the very program we want to see. If you've ever done this, you know how frustrating it is.

115

We finally decided to do something about this. So we created a "We're Just Too Tired to Talk" media shelf, where we keep blank tapes, DVDs, a felt-tip pen, labels, and a section for previously recorded programs.

Now, when we want to tape a program, we know where we can find a tape or DVD for recording. We label it and date it before we record, and afterward, we immediately place it on our media shelf. As a result, when we are really bummed out, we're already prepared for a "Just Too Tired to Talk" Date.

HAVE DINNER DELIVERED:
Sometimes we order pizza to eat while we watch our videos or DVDs. We keep a couple of current pizza coupons on our media shelf so it won't take much energy to find them. Other times we pull out frozen dinners and plop them in the microwave. We don't go out of the house and we don't talk to each other unless we want to. Another tip—we don't answer the phone during this time. Instead, we let the voice mail collect messages.

CONSIDER ANOTHER OPTION:
Our friends Jon and Maria told us about their favorite "We're Just Too Tired to Talk" Date, which does require one last spurt of energy. They go to the video/DVD store and then get take-out food from their favorite Chinese restaurant. When they get home, they roll the television and DVD player into their bedroom and crawl into bed with their bed trays and Chinese dinner.

They eat, watch movies, and fall asleep — whatever they want to do. And they don't talk unless they want to. The next morning, life continues with conversation, and one of the things they talk about is their relaxing date the night before.

42
LONG-DISTANCE FAX-A-DATE

THE IDEA:

What do you do when you are on the road and you're tired and lonely? Although we travel a lot together, there are times when one of us is on the road alone. It's not fun — especially over the weekend!

Sometimes you just have to make the best of a situation. We may be miles apart, but we've discovered how to Fax-a-Date.

The goal of a Fax-a-Date is to stay in touch. It also gives us something to look forward to. Most hotels have Fax facilities for their guests, so after we've completed our evening speaking engagement or seminar, we are ready to begin having Fax fun!

FAX THEN PHONE:

You can use your own creativity, but here are a few ideas to get you started.

◆ How do I love you, let me fax the ways . . .

◆ The funniest thing that happened to me today was . . .

◆ My most favorite thing about you is . . .

After we've exchanged a couple of faxes, we follow up with a phone call. Phone calls are nice, but there is something about faxing notes back and forth that is fun.

FIND OTHER WAYS TO STAY CLOSE:
If you don't have access to a fax machine, don't rule out this date. There are other ways you can connect and stay in touch. Why not:

◆ E-mail back and forth.
◆ Read the same article or chapter in a book and be prepared to discuss it when you call each other at the end of the day or when you return home.
◆ Hide a love note in your mate's briefcase, suitcase, or garment bag.
◆ Watch the same television program and then talk about it.
◆ Plan your next vacation or a twenty-four-hour getaway.
◆ Talk through your schedule for the next week.
◆ Plan a special date with each other in the next ten days.

Long-Distance Dates encourage us when we are tired and lonely. They keep us in touch and help us to appreciate each other in a new way. But the best part of being separated by the miles is getting on that plane or train or in that car and coming home to our mate. For a great Welcome-Home Date see the Limo Date (Date 47).

43

OVERCOMING-
THE-BLAHS
DATE

THE IDEA:

If you're like us, you feel just too tired to date when the blahs are getting you down. The weather may be too hot or too cold or too rainy. Your finances may resemble the national debt. Your to-do list may seem endless. That's enough to make anyone tired.

Maybe you need to take time out for an Overcoming-the-Blahs Date. You can do one of two things.

CHASE AWAY SOMEONE ELSE'S BLAHS:

Do something to cheer up somebody else. When we get involved in doing something for someone else, the blahs quickly disappear. Consider the following:

◆ Together with your mate, take an evening and call or write someone you haven't contacted in a while. Recently, we got a letter from an Austrian friend we haven't heard from in years. It made our day.

◆ Write a note of encouragement to someone you know who is having a problem.

120

◆ Make a date to visit a nursing home or hospital. Many people in these institutions rarely get visitors and could use a little encouragement.

◆ Brighten the life of an elderly friend or relative by making a surprise visit. Call ahead if you're not sure he or she is up to a surprise.

STEP OUT OF YOUR COMFORT ZONE:
Do something out of character and unusual. You may want to:

◆ Try a new recipe—something different from anything you've ever tried before.

◆ If you have a fireplace, build a fire and roast hot dogs.

◆ Have a picnic on the living room floor. All you need is a checkered tablecloth, French bread, and cold cuts. Why not put in some colored hard-boiled eggs? This will add some laughter as you chase the blahs away.

◆ Get out some of your young children's games— Twister is a good one—and play the games together. Or go Rollerblading, if you haven't already tried this sport.

You may enjoy these dates so much that you find yourself looking forward to the next time a case of the blahs strikes.

44

SHOWERS, BUBBLE BATHS, AND CANDLES DATE

THE IDEA:

Recently, we spoke at a sweetheart banquet. As is our custom at the end of our talk, we asked the group to tell us about their favorite dates. When we do this, we usually get the best dating suggestions after the formal program. This time was no exception. One older couple stood around until we were alone and then shared the following story.

"When we were first married, we attended a marriage seminar where someone shared about how much fun it is to shower together. We tried it and found out they were right. We've been showering together every morning since! We didn't know if we should share that with the whole group."

TAKE A WATER BREAK:

This is a good date suggestion for the times you and your mate are just too tired to do anything else. A shower really soothes and refreshes. Another couple offers this variation.

"We both work long hours. Sometimes when we come home we are totally exhausted. We wouldn't even have the energy to shower together, so here's what we do. Fortunately, we have two bathrooms (and no children yet), so we run each other's baths in separate bathrooms. We add scented bath oil beads or bubble bath — whatever we know our mate likes. We also light candles for each other. Votive candles work great. We turn on soothing music and know we are both in for a relaxing treat.

"It's fun to indulge in the quietness of a warm bath that someone else has prepared for you. We've even decided it's okay if the warm water saps what little energy we might still have. This is a "We're Just Too Tired" Date, so we have no expectations for the evening except to relax and be together. Anything else that happens is totally spontaneous and optional."

Which do you prefer — showers or baths? Maybe you have your own private whirlpool. When you are just too tired, take your pick!

THE
BEST DATES
FROM MARRIAGE
ALIVE ALUMNI

45
HIKING DATE

THE IDEA:

Our best dates usually have one thing in common—few distractions and lots of conversation. Walking together is a great way to accomplish this. Of course, when walking in the mountains, you are allowed to refer to this activity as hiking. (Calling it hiking also justifies purchasing hiking boots, day packs, and trail mix with chocolate candy!)

Marriage Alive alumni Sam and Cindy love to hike in the Smoky Mountains and have told us about their experiences.

MAP OUT A WEEKEND:

"One of our favorite hikes starts on Friday night," Sam told us. "That's when we take the kids over to Cindy's parents' house. Her parents also consider this to be somewhat of a wilderness adventure.

"We get an early start on Saturday morning and stop on the way for breakfast. After breakfast, we realize something is missing! No sticky feeling from syrup kisses, no food impregnated on our clothing, and most of all, no stares throughout the meal from the entire nonsmoking section of the restaurant. We agree that this missing feeling is good and should be encountered on a regular basis.

"Arriving at the trailhead, we begin our four-mile hike along the Appalachian Trail to Charles Bunion. No, this isn't a discount shoe store in Pigeon Forge. It is a scenic overlook that makes a nice spot for lunch. The distance and difficulty also make this an enjoyable day hike. A day pack is all we need to carry water and lunch."

ENLIGHTEN YOUR LOVED ONE AS YOU HIKE:
"Hiking should be a requirement for all marriages. It provides the husband with the unique opportunity to enlighten his wife through expressions of deep philosophical truths. I can't describe the impact this has on Cindy as I share my analogies to life. 'I think my life is like a mountain spruce, balding from acid rain,' really touches her. She is so moved, at times she can't even look at me. She simply stares up in the sky shaking her head. I must overwhelm her.

"Cindy's only disappointment with our first hiking experience was that there was no hotel along the trail anywhere.

"Being the alert and sensitive husband I am, I suggested we stay overnight in a backcountry shelter our next trip. Once again, she stared up at the sky and started shaking her head. I did hear her say something about God. I suppose she was thanking Him for me."

By the way, Sam and Cindy just took a refresher Marriage Alive seminar. We are happy to report their next date will be a romantic date. Cindy agreed to go to any backcountry shelter that has a Jacuzzi!

46
BREAKFAST-
ON-A-MOTORCYCLE
DATE

THE IDEA:

We have always enjoyed Breakfast Dates. When our three sons were teenagers, it was a niche of time we found that we could slip out by ourselves and get back home before the first sleepyhead even woke up.

Over the years, we've tried many different places for our Breakfast Dates, but none were quite as creative as the place Bob and Betty chose.

Bob and Betty are your typical dual-career couple with a time-crunch lifestyle that leaves them few opportunities for finding time alone as a couple. Bob decided to do something about it, and thus their unique Breakfast Date.

CREATE YOUR OWN PLACE:

The day started as an average day. Bob left early for work in order to meet an important deadline—or so Betty thought. After a quick cup of coffee, Betty was on her way to her downtown office. After parking her car, she began the two-block walk to her office. Thinking about her daily agenda, she hardly noticed the commotion at the next intersection.

Then she saw him. There was Bob with his parked

motorcycle. But this was not an ordinary parked motorcycle! It had been transformed into a most creative sidewalk café!

The motorcycle was covered with a tablecloth, complete with two place settings of dishes, a thermos of coffee, and sweet rolls. Needless to say, this provided laughs for those who walked by, as well as a reminder to spend time with those you love.

You may not own a motorcycle, but don't let that stop you. Plan your own unique Breakfast Date. Take it from us. It's a great way to start the day!

THE LIMO
DATE

THE IDEA:

We will never forget our first ride in a limo. Our first book had just been published, and, as guests of our publisher, we were attending a bookseller's convention in Washington, D.C. The real thrill for these two green writers was sharing the limo ride to the hotel with a seasoned author. Besides recognizing her name, we knew she was seasoned by her luggage. She had only one carry-on!

Limos can add excitement to any date. But they are also expensive, so if you're not running over with money, take our friend's suggestion and improvise.

ECONOMIZE AND STILL HAVE FUN:

Judy had spent the entire week at the bedside of her mother. To say the week had been stressful is an understatement. On the flight home, she wondered if her husband, Dan (who is not time oriented), would be there to meet her. Was he ever!

As Judy deplaned, she heard her name on the pager: "Mrs. Roberts, please meet your party at Gate 6."

This is odd, she thought, as she looked around for Dan. About that time she spotted her husband. There he was, complete with a driver's cap and a huge sign that said, "Limo for Mrs. Judy Roberts."

He escorted her to the parking lot. Their station wagon wasn't exactly a limo, but as Dan loaded her luggage in the back, she felt special anyway.

By the way, they did not go straight home. Instead Dan whisked her away for a surprise date. Where did they go? You'll have to use your imagination!

Several hours later, Judy arrived home, relaxed and ready to catch up with her two teenage sons, help her ten-year-old daughter with a history project, and eat home-delivered pizza.

48

AIRPORT
DATE

THE IDEA:

Airports have always fascinated us. We have experienced some really dramatic and traumatic things at airports.

Four days before our wedding, I (Claudia) met Dave's parents and sister for the first time in the Atlanta airport. They had flown in from Naples, Italy, where Dave's dad was stationed with the army.

Our most joyous and most tiring airport experience was in the airport at Frankfurt, Germany, back in our army days. I (Dave), at the invitation of Uncle Sam, arrived in Germany three months ahead of Claudia. Needless to say, we were eager to be together again. Claudia's twenty-four-hour flight was on one of those old army prop planes. It arrived twelve hours late, after stopping for repairs and refueling in Newfoundland. Claudia still remembers wondering if she would make it to Germany.

Our most traumatic airport experience was losing our five-year-old in the Atlanta airport minutes before we were to board our plane for Vienna, where we were living at that time. Another time, as Claudia flew back to Europe with our three young sons, an engine went out, causing the flight to return to New York for an emergency landing.

With all our airport traumas, we were naturally curious when Marriage Alive alumni, Bill and Jean, told us that their favorite dates were at airports.

USE YOUR IMAGINATION:

"When we were first married, our dating budget was practically nonexistent, so we had to rely on our own ingenuity. One thing we loved doing was going to the Detroit metropolitan airport to watch people and planes come and go.

"Sometimes we took a snack or soda to have while we people-and-plane watched. We would rejoice with people whose loved ones were coming home and cry with those whose loved ones were leaving. It was during the Vietnam conflict, so there were a lot of sad departures, but also quite a few emotional and joyful arrivals.

"As we watched others, we would fantasize about their destinations and imagine ourselves traveling to faraway places. We'd wonder what people would be like and what we would do if we were traveling to Florida, Hawaii, Europe, or New York. As young newlyweds with lots of dreams, it was a fun, inexpensive date."

The tightened airport security since 9/11 makes the kind . of airport date Bill and Jean had more difficult—but not impossible. You just have to modify it a bit. Now you can watch people come and go in the baggage claim area of the airport lobby, right before the security checkpoint.

We spend a lot of time in airports since we lead seminars around the country and in Europe. When our flights are delayed, we enjoy people-watching, and while we are waiting for our luggage to arrive, from time to time, we will pretend we are meeting each other. It's fun to run into each other's arms and hug and kiss as we say hello. Did you realize an airport is one place you can kiss passionately in public and get away with it? So the next time you're stuck in an airport, use your own creativity and have an airport date!

SURPRISE-TRAVEL DATE

THE IDEA:

One misconception about traveling is that it is always exciting and fun. We must admit at times it can be, but more often than not, life on the road is just living without the convenience of home and with many added frustrations.

Recently, we were flying to speak at an army installation in Wisconsin. We like to use our time wisely, so we had planned to work on the plane. The only problem was one of us sat in the front of the plane and the other in the back, making it hard to communicate.

On the trip home, our flight left Minneapolis late. We were afraid we were going to miss our connection in Memphis. But the connecting flight was two hours late arriving in Memphis.

Fun? That day traveling was about as much fun as cleaning the oven!

CREATE YOUR OWN SURPRISE:

When our friends Jody and Linda lived in Vienna, they traveled extensively in Europe and the Orient. They also had to deal with the frustrating little surprises of travel. But on one particular trip, Jody decided to create his own surprise that was anything but frustrating. He planned and pulled off a Surprise-Travel Date.

TAKE A DIFFERENT TURN:

"It was to be a long, long trip," Linda told us. "First, we were booked on a flight to London, and then on to Hong Kong. Taking care of last-minute details for our month absence from our home in Vienna left me totally exhausted. All I wanted to do on the first leg of our trip was to sleep.

"Imagine my surprise when Jody handed me a home-made card. My creative husband had written me a poem. Now, I said he was creative, not necessarily poetic, but this poem took the prize. He invited me to spend two days alone with him in London.

"Jody had made reservations at a wonderful English inn. He also presented me with tickets for a play we had wanted to see. I felt like he had given me the moon!"

MAKE THE MOST OF THE MOMENT:

"The first thing we did after we arrived in London was to take a nap and enjoy the luxury of having no schedule to meet, no one to call, and nothing to do. We just relaxed and enjoyed being together.

"I can't tell you what a difference this Surprise-Travel Date made in my attitude about this trip and about life in general. I still savor the memory of Jody's thoughtfulness and the wonderful way he expressed his love and commitment to me on that trip. We highly recommend a Surprise-Travel Date to all who can pull it off."

MAKE IT HAPPEN:

You may not be traveling to Europe or the Orient, but even if it's only three hours down the road, consider taking your mate along. Since we travel together leading Marriage Alive seminars, it's easy to tack on another day or two. It doesn't cost that much more, and what we get from our time alone is well worth it. It's fun if one of you can pull it off as a surprise, but either way, it's a great way to travel. Just ask Jody and Linda!

50
BIRTHDAY
TREASURE-HUNT
DATE

THE IDEA:

Birthday surprises aren't always pleasant! I (Claudia) have never forgotten the year no one remembered my birthday all day long. Claiming I had a headache, I slipped into bed early to end this awful, terrible day. No sooner had I fallen asleep than the doorbell rang. You guessed it. There were all of our friends with a surprise birthday.

Years later, we went away for a weekend to celebrate Claudia's birthday. This may be hard to believe, but I (Dave) actually forgot it was her birthday the day it came. At eleven in the morning, Claudia, tired of feeling angry and rejected, finally told me what was bothering her.

Some of our Marriage Alive alumni, like Judy and Bob, outdo us. Judy described how she surprised Bob with a Birthday Treasure-Hunt Date. Here's how she described it.

CREATE CLUES:

"It wasn't even Bob's birthday. Actually, it was Sunday afternoon, the day before Bob's birthday, so I would catch him off guard. His first clue that something was up came when I handed him an envelope with a clue inside. My one-of-a-kind poetic clue let him know the hunt was beginning immediately. No need to change clothes—he could proceed to the first location.

"His clues took him all over our neighborhood and a surrounding four-mile radius. One of his clues was a phone call from me that he received in a phone booth. Another clue took him to a grocery store to buy his own birthday balloon.

"The next clue led him to my dad's home. Laid out for him in their guest bedroom was a change of clothes to dress for dinner. The final treasure stop was our favorite restaurant where I, and two other couples, greeted him. We had a wonderful evening celebrating his birthday together. That was one birthday he didn't even mind getting a year older!"

CHOOSE THE BEST TIME:
If your mate has a birthday coming up and he or she likes adventure, consider a Birthday Treasure-Hunt Date. Just don't plan it when his or her favorite football, baseball, or basketball team is playing on television. And plan to have this date before bedtime!

51
ALONE-AND-
TOGETHER
DATE

THE IDEA:

Is it possible to be too close to your mate? Most couples complain of not having enough time with each other. On the other end of the spectrum are couples like us who are together almost continuously.

At times we simply need a break from each other, so we really appreciated the dating suggestion from Marriage Alive alumni David and Susanne. They suggested that we have an Alone-and-Together Date. This is also a great date for couples who aren't together all the time, but do need time alone.

Here's how David and Susanne described one of their Alone-and-Together Dates.

MAKE A DAY OF IT:

"One of our favorite dates is an all-day trip to the mountains. We pack a picnic lunch and go to our spot by the stream. We spend most of the afternoon separately. With three small children and a medical practice, our lives are busy, hectic, and at times quite stressful. We both need time alone, so this gives us a chance to read, pray, journal, hike, nap—whatever we individually feel like doing.

"Later in the afternoon, we meet back at our spot and share our thoughts, insights, and any discoveries we have made, like pretty rocks, flowers, or mushrooms. It's amazing how these things come back into perspective when we take time together and alone to reflect and just enjoy being out in nature.

"On the way home, we stop at a favorite restaurant for dinner. Our three children, tired babysitter, and hectic pace of life are all waiting for us when we get home; but we have discovered after our Alone-and-Together Date that we are refreshed and ready to face the next challenge."

52

TEN BONUS DATES FOR MATES

MORE DATES:

Because our Marriage Alive alumni are so creative and have so much fun dating their mates, we couldn't possibly include all their terrific dating suggestions. We have squeezed in as many as possible, however, by condensing ten more dates for mates from our Marriage Alive graduates.

1. "We love to go to a deserted field, take a picnic, and fly kites as we listen to classical music on our CD player."—Bob and Cindy

2. "Craft shows and antiquing are our favorite dates. We always try to stop on the way home to watch the sunset."—Chip and Susan

3. "Our favorite date was a four-day cruise on the Chesapeake Bay on a chartered thirty-two-foot sailboat."—Bill and Val

4. "One of our favorite dates is a day away to escape the responsibilities of parenting for a few hours and just

to be silly and do whatever we want to do. It's fun to go to a state fair or an amusement park. We love riding the bumper cars." — Bill and Donna

5. "Skiing together is fun, exhilarating, and brings color to your cheeks. Don't forget to have a snowball fight!" — Jay and Alison

6. "We love the great outdoors and backpacking and camping out." — Hans and Barbara

7. "Cooking breakfast at our favorite waterfall is invigorating. If we're early enough, we get to see the sun rise." — Greg and Cheryl

8. "After early church, we take the Sunday paper and a picnic lunch on our ski boat. We motor into a deserted cove, put our feet up, read the paper, and just relax." — Kent and Susan

9. "We love to go to our favorite little restaurant, order coffee and dessert, and enjoy the live jazz music." — Janet and John

10. "We enjoy reliving our first date with each other. We go to the same place we first went together, eat the same food, watch the same movie, and talk about the feelings we shared that day and how we have grown in our relationship since then." — Patty and Bill

ABOUT THE AUTHORS

Claudia Arp and David Arp, MSW, a husband-wife team, are founders and directors of Marriage Alive International, a groundbreaking program providing marriage-and-family building resources for the church and community. Their Marriage Alive seminars are popular across the U.S. and in Europe. They are popular speakers, seminar leaders, columnists, and authors of numerous books and video curricula including *Answering the 8 Cries of the Spirited Child*, the *10 Great Dates* series, and the Gold Medallion Award–winning *The Second Half of Marriage*. Frequent contributors to print and broadcast media, the Arps have appeared on NBC *Today*, CBS *This Morning*, Public Television and *Focus on the Family*. The Arps have been married for over forty years and live in Great Falls, Virginia.

Marriage Alive International, Inc.

Marriage Alive International, Inc., founded by husband-wife team Claudia and David Arp, MSW, is a nonprofit marriage-and-family enrichment ministry dedicated to providing resources, seminars, and training to empower churches to help build better marriages and families. Marriage Alive also works with community organizations, the U.S. military, schools, and businesses.

The Arps are marriage and family educators and have been involved in marriage ministry in the USA and in Europe for more than twenty-five years. Their Marriage Alive seminars are popular across the U.S. and in Europe.

The mission of Marriage Alive is to train and empower leaders who invest in others by building strong marriage and family relationships through the integration of biblical truth, contemporary research, practical application, and fun.

Marriage Alive resources and services include:

♦ Marriage and family books in eight languages

♦ Video-based educational programs, including *10 Great Dates to Energize Your Marriage* and *Second Half of Marriage*

♦ Premarriage, marriage, and parenting seminars including *Before You Say "I Do," Marriage Alive,* and *Second Half of Marriage* seminars.

♦ Consulting, training, leadership development, coaching, and mentoring

Contact Marriage Alive at www.marriagealive.com or (888) 690-6667.
Sign up for the free Marriage Builder e-mail newsletter at www.marriagealive.com.